The Facilitative Leader
Leadership in the VUCA Era

Sanjay Dugar

STARDOM BOOKS

STARDOM BOOKS

WORLDWIDE

www.StardomBooks.com

STARDOM BOOKS

A Division of Stardom Publishing

and infoYOGIS Technologies.

105-501 Silverside Road

Wilmington, DE 19809

Copyright © 2018 by Stardom Publishing.

All rights reserved, including right to reproduce this book or portions thereof in any form whatsoever.

FIRST EDITION NOVEMBER 2018

Stardom Books

The Facilitative Leader/
Leadership in the VUCA Era.

Sanjay Dugar

p. cm.

Category: Self-help / Leadership

ISBN-13: 978-1-7323287-6-1

ISBN-10: 1-7323287-6-5

DEDICATION

To my father – Late Shri. Jaswanth Mull Dugar
To my mother – Late Smt. Ugama Devi Dugar
To my father-in-law – Late Shri. Subhash C Jain
for all their sacrifices, blessings, and guidance

CONTENTS

INTRODUCTION   1

PART ONE: LEADERSHIP EVOLUTION   5

1. HOW LEADERSHIP HAS EVOLVED?   7
2. WHAT IS THE CHANGE IN THE ENVIRONMENT TODAY?   37
3. WHAT WOULD BE A MORE SUITABLE METHOD OF LEADING TODAY?   45

PART TWO: SOUNDS LIKE THE COMPETENCIES OF A FACILITATOR   51

4. THE COMPETENCIES REQUIRED OF A LEADER, MATCHES THAT OF A FACILITATOR   55
5. SCENARIOS WHERE THEY CAN BE DEPLOYED EFFECTIVELY   73
6. TIPS, TOOLS, AND TECHNIQUES   79
7. THREE STORIES   109

PART THREE: COMPETENT FACILITATORS ARE NATURAL LEADERS   121

8. IS IT REALLY A NEW SKILL?   123
9. IT CAN BE LEARNED EASILY   129

10. ADDITIONAL RESOURCES 135

11. CONCLUSION: TODAY'S LEADERS NEED TO
    BE GREAT FACILITATORS 137

ACKNOWLEDGMENTS

With the blessings of Goddess Sarasvati, the Hindu Goddess of knowledge, music, art, wisdom, and learning, this book came into existence.

I need to start by thanking my awesome wife Preeti Dugar, who has been my inspiration, and has helped with taking care of so many things and free my time to write, which was so important to help me focus. The sacrifices you have made for me mean a lot. Thank you very much.

My three adorable children, my son-in-law Tilak Ajmera, my daughter Poorvi Dugar Ajmera, and my son Vardhan Dugar, who have been able to take time from their work to go over my drafts and provide good feedback, deeply appreciate their time and effort. Thank you for the support.

I am blessed with a very supportive family of in-laws, mother-in-law Smt. Kanta Jain, brother-in-law, Shri. Peeyush Jain, his wife Smt. Namrata Jain, my nephew Karneet, my niece Minolae, their support in everything I do, and in every way possible. One could not ask for more. Thank you so much for being with me at all times.

My enthusiastic and absolutely rocking team at C2C Organizational Development Pvt. Ltd. for helping me gather so much information and encouraging me along the way, and providing me with some good illustrations. A thank you alone is not enough, my heartfelt gratitude to all of you at C2COD.

My publishing team, led by Raam Anand, whose words of encouragement kept me going at the desired pace, without which this book may not have been put together at all. The support in editing, creating illustrations, cover design, and most importantly publishing it. Truly appreciate the support and a huge thank you to the entire team at Stardom.

FOREWORD

There is an abundance of literature that describes the role of the leader as a 'hero', leading from the front, giving direction and modelling the way. There is also a plethora that describe the leader as a 'servant', being there to support the team in their moment of need, lifting the hearts of those who are struggling. Both of these metaphors are now being surpassed with the leader as the 'host', the facilitative leader that creates the space for the team, function and entire organisation to interact and having the ability to step forward and intervene in the process when needed and also comfortable in stepping back too.

This new generation of facilitative leadership is essential in helping create an environment where people can flourish whilst all around them is volatile and complex. It's not sufficient to have smart individuals to make transformation a success it's also crucial that interaction and collaboration between people and teams is at its optimum....it's not what's between the ears that counts, it's what's between the noses! This is the domain of facilitative leadership.

With so many years' experience in the IT industry along with being a Certified Professional Facilitator (CPF), Sanjay is perfectly positioned to describe the realities of operating in a volatile and complex world and seeing how the power of facilitation can help teams come together and play a part in transformation.

This book will be seen as an important milestone and is an essential read for leaders who are seeking to explore the power of facilitation as a role and a skillset that can be adopted to bring about transformational change. It also provides a solid insight to facilitators who are keen to see how the competencies of a facilitator can be brought to bear in complex change.

    Trevor Durnford
    Global Chair
    International Association of Facilitators (IAF)

INTRODUCTION

HELP! My ways of leading are not working!!

An informal meeting with John (name changed for privacy reasons), a senior corporate leader of a large technology company in India, was sitting at the far end of a coffee shop, to avoid getting bothered by the din in the place. I was bang on time, 6:00 pm sharp, which was very much an ingrained habit of mine, a habit that I was and I am proud of too. I recognized him quite easily as I had seen his LinkedIn profile which had his very recent picture. His checked shirt and chinos made him look very business-like compared to most others around who were in jeans and tees. He was looking at his watch and sipping his coffee, clearly waiting for me to come. As I walked over to his table, he got up from his chair and extended his hand, and he opened the conversation with "Help! My ways of leading are not working!!"

I was meeting with John, to possibly take on the role of an Executive Coach to him, and, was expecting him to ask me questions about my coaching abilities and experiences. I was so taken aback, that all I could do was stay silent and to make sure that my jaw does not drop. I was at a total loss of words with this unexpected opening statement that even preceded the hello and the usual introductions.

In the awkward silence that followed, John was quick to notice the situation, and with an apologetical look on his face, he said, "Look, I have spoken to some of your references that you gave, and I am already convinced that I would want you to coach me. Hence, I directly started with my problem statement."

Having regained my composure, from the mind state that I was in, I managed to give him a smile of sorts, that I think put him into a little bit of ease. I also realized that this

1

problem was a very serious situation for him. He responded with the same statement again, though with a lot more controlled tone, "My ways of leading are not working, and I need you to help me find my way out of this. I quickly need to get back to being the excellent leader that I am known to be."

I was still thinking over the words that were said, and mulling over this thought in my mind - one of the most respected leaders, a great orator, often addressing conferences as a keynote speaker, making this statement, is this really true? I noticed the stress in his eyes, and the unusually dark shadows beneath them, and his tone conveyed a lot of anxiety. It almost sounded like a desperate call that is looking for that one last option.

Being a bit of an analytical type of person who does not very easily show emotions, I quickly recovered from this state, to casually say "Can we please start at the beginning, and tell me what this is all about?"

This perhaps made him very comfortable, and he looked straight into my eyes, like the confident leader that he was, although much in defiance of his current state of affairs, he started to share his story.

"My team engagement pulse and 360 feedback, that was always at best in the company for so many years has started to decline considerably in the last three quarters and I am worried that it could only get worse, unless I change something, though I do not know what is it that I need to change. I also have started feeling this personally, as I do not see myself capable of aligning my team towards the goal, and to create the required environment for them to perform at the level I know they can. I had very confidently declared to the Board of Directors a level of performance that I would get, and they backed me with all these large investments," he said.

After a brief pause, he continued, "three quarters have gone by, I have had multiple meetings with the team, and there does not seem any way forward. I have my team members giving a variety of excuses for not completing their tasks, which I know is not exactly true. I have tried various ways to give feedback, guide them, coach them, but somehow nothing seems to work."

He looked at me as if searching for some emotional solace, and as he saw me nodding while listening intently to what he was saying, he continued on.

"My neck is on the block now. I am not so much worried about that, although I can kick myself for over committing; my real concern is that I know this team is smart, has the potential, and can deliver, and that if they did it would be beneficial to everyone. I also know that there is something I am doing wrong, or not doing something that I should be doing, which will help draw out the full that hidden potential of the team."

Seeing the situation, and sensing his emotional state, I responded with some initial probing to also let him know that I understand the depth of the situation; and after the usual contracting of a coaching assignment, he stepped into the transformational journey. After seven sessions, covering about 14 hours of coaching, with meetings in his office, his home, and in some coffee shops, he figured a way out that would work for him.

He was back on track.

A few months after these coaching sessions, I happened to run into him at the airport lounge, and that meeting was such a contrast to the first one. He was excitedly sharing the changes he had made to his ways of working with people, how he now could get everyone to share their views early in the game to make quick, aligned, and collective decisions. He spoke about the joy he was seeing amongst his team members even when they were stretching to get things done, and how confident he was feeling about his ability to lead now. This new-found confidence and emotional state were such a delight to see. John had made my day.

I have come across many such similar situations from a variety of leaders across various types of organizations, across various levels of hierarchy. Large mature organizations to start-ups, especially so in the last year or two; have all gone through these situations, and in my journey of helping them overcome these situations, I have had some learnings and thoughts. I have also observed some patterns emerge. Studying some of the research papers on leadership, coupled with some additional research that I took up, interviewing several successful corporate leaders of today; I thought it would be useful to share my findings in the form of a book – The Facilitative Leader. I strongly believe that this book could help leaders significantly.

PART ONE: LEADERSHIP EVOLUTION

Leadership has gone through a change based on the needs related to the stage that the world was in at that time. Historically, we have seen the emergence of leadership from the Personality Era, Influence Era, Transformational Era, all being triggered by situations in the environment. Many authors have published articles and books around them. There are also many research papers around these. I am only discussing in detail these specific eras, as there was significant evolution and changed behaviors that could help us understand the development of leadership.

Each of this evolution that has taken place has been based on changes in the environment to which the leadership approach had to match and fulfill the need based on the situation, for the leader to excel.

It would be valuable to understand this evolution and the context that brought about this evolution, to determine what is it that is creating the need for the next significant change.

With the current stage of accelerated change to address the VUCA situation, we are now moving to the **Facilitator Era**.

At the end of this part, a suitable approach based on the current situation is presented, which builds a convincing case that a new Era – the **Facilitator Era**, has come, and those that can skill up to meet this need, are the leaders that would excel.

1
HOW LEADERSHIP HAS EVOLVED?

At the airport, having checked in for my flight back home, after a good four consecutive days of traveling across multiple destinations, I was impatiently waiting at the gate, standing in the queue along with others who were as impatient as me. There was a buzz of activity at the counter ahead of us, and I was wondering what was going on. Suddenly, the sound system starts with a crackle, and a woman's voice comes alive to say that my flight is delayed by four hours with the new ETD showing 03:00 hours. Of course, the reason cited for the delay is always very vague, and in this case too, the familiar announcement was made – "delayed due to the late arrival of the incoming flight." I was upset, but quickly resigned to the fate and reconciled with myself to make the most of the time I had before me now. Already weary with the multi-city travel, all I could do was let out a sigh. I did not have the energy to go around the shops at the airport that was trying to attract me with big sale signs and discount offers, with impeccably dressed sales girls. Feeling too tired to go and find out what was really going on about the delay, and seeing the people at the gate counter expressing their annoyance in very loud voices, and the soft voice of the customer relations executive there trying to stay calm as much as she could, I also realized that it would be pointless for me to add to that crowd.

I just curled up on one of those recliner seats. I dug out some reading material that I had stashed away in my laptop backpack and started to read some of the research papers on leadership styles, that I had printed out last week, but not had the time to read them. As I was reading these research papers, a few questions I found myself asking were, Why are the leadership styles changing? What is causing this change? Does this mean that leadership methods would change again? While grappling with these questions, another thought around the time dimension crept into my mind – "Have we reached the point where the next evolution is needed?" The more I ran these questions in my mind, and the recent situations where I was helping a few leaders, I was convinced that it was about time. This was the trigger that got me to start writing this book.

It is said that you get good lessons from history, to be able to plan for the present and the future; especially if they are analyzed well to see the advantages and limitations, we can learn from it and come up with a plan that would work for the present and the future. I thus, thought it apt to briefly collate and describe this evolution from various research that I had read, and share some salient points from them. While we shall not dwell too much into the very distant past, we will certainly look at the recent ones more closely, to help guide us towards the proposed new approach to be able to lead more effectively now on. Perhaps, as we go through the salient points, it would help you connect better if you can visualize some leaders that you may have come across in our lives, at some place, and at some point in time, thereby making it real for yourself, and would perhaps explain these thoughts even more clearly than what just words can do.

The Personality Era.

The first among the "formal" corporate leadership styles that emerged from various research studies talk about personality as an appeal that could influence a group of people to align and do things that the influencer wanted to be done. Some of it was explained as based on "the Great Man (or Woman)" and some others based on their "Traits" that attracted people to trust them and work with them – almost like blind faith.

A little incident in my life that explains this.

I was very excited as a nine-year-old boy that I now became a big brother to a baby sister. I was even more ecstatic on that summer day – May 11, 1973, when I was to go and see this little live baby doll. Here I was, prancing along, one hand in my father's firm grip, and my other hand holding on to a toy that I had bought for my baby sister.

As soon as I entered the room, I pulled out my hand from my father and ran to the bedside, and was amazed at what I saw – a tiny little baby, so small, big eyes that were tightly shut, fast asleep, and all wrapped up in a warm towel – I just gazed at her, and so many dreams flashed through my mind – my sister and I would do this, and do that, and this went on and on. I was brought back to reality when I heard the feeble voice of my mother, asking me how I was. Without caring to reply, I blurted, look how small she is, isn't she cute? And my mother quietly gave me a broad smile.

The next few days were etched in my memory, as I saw my sister feeling very comfortable and secure when my mother was around, and even her cries would stop the moment she felt the hand of my mother on her. This further grew as she got comfortable with my father and me as well, but certainly not as much as she trusted my mother.

Time went on, and in very many situations I found how she would accept to do difficult things or even things that she did not like; no amount of coaxing her or even bribing her to do it from me would help, but If my mother just told her to do it, she would readily accept and not only do them but do them well. We all feel that need to follow a leader that makes us feel safe.

We all do feel that need for safety even in our corporate worlds. So many decades later, I still see this kind of impact in certain situations, where some comfort, some assurance, some signal from a leader we trust; that drives us to give our best to the tasks we are doing. All because the leader makes us feel safe.

Let's look at the environment where this type of leadership flourished.

At the time when basic needs of food and shelter for many was not assured, and the safety of their family was always a question in the minds of many, correlating to the bottom two layers of Maslow's Hierarchy of Needs – namely the physiological and safety layers, it is evident that the leaders who could make people feel safe would be the ones they looked up to. Much like the little baby waiting for the secure feel of the mother.

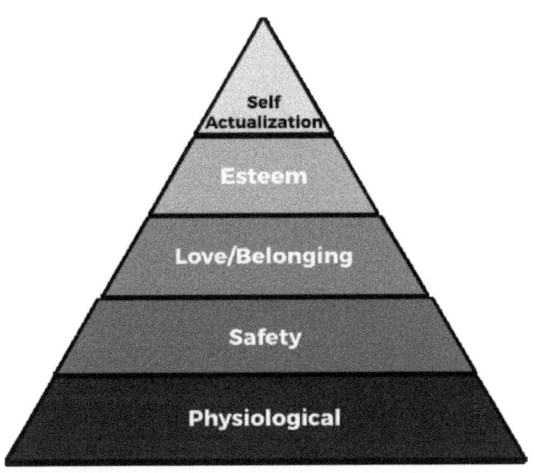

Even if these leaders had some shortcomings, people chose to look the other side, and for their own security and safety, they would remain loyal. Most often these leaders were themselves owners of businesses, where they had brought in the resource that was scarce – Money. It was easy to get people, and it was equally easy to get their products accepted in the market, as product choices and availability were also limited. All the marketing messages were around availability, and often you had to pre-book and receive the products as and when they got made. Advertising that bookings were open was quite common. When what you have is in demand, it is a lot easier to be a leader.

And of course, as the situation around started to change, this type of leadership quickly faded away.

With physiological and safety needs becoming easy to secure, as more and more organizations found ways to build this in, like salary levels, rewards for higher productivity, wellness schemes, and other such monetary incentives, this style of leadership proved to be too simplistic, and leadership in the corporate world, now needed to take a new turn, mainly if they wanted to get the right workforce in, and to be able to compete in the newly opening up markets. Leadership methods had to adapt to this change. It had to evolve into the next era.

Here is a little space for you to capture or reflect upon a story of yours, where you recollect the power and usefulness of a leader whose personality awed you.

The leader's name:

What were your needs at that time:

The incident:

The Influence Era.

With people soon realizing that leaders cannot be identified based only on their characteristics or traits, and their being able to provide safety; rather it became more important to relate with the people they lead. In other words, the leader's role needed to become a two-way connect for them to hold their position among the people they lead. Their communication needed to create that bond with the people so that they are keen to follow the thoughts and actions of the leader. This logically then morphed into the era where leaders became successful leaders based on their ability to influence others. Of course, they did find different ways and means to influence their employees, to suit their personal styles and ways of working.

People already sensing their security was assured, were now seeking the next step in the Maslow's Hierarchy – love/belonging. The former leadership methods came across as authoritarian, dictatorial, and controlling styles, which was now not appealing to people anymore. A clear shift.

It was being recognized that it was not just the act of the leader in building safety or the characteristics and traits that would drive people to do things for them. Leadership was shifting to be able to inspire people and influence them to strive towards a set goal or goals. The leader, therefore, needs to be a strong communicator that would touch the heart of the team members, and that was the best way to get them aligned towards the objectives while also answering their question around the WIIFM – What's in it for me?.

One such incident that I recall from my school life.

I was a student in one of the best schools in Bangalore, India, Baldwin Boys High School, my Alma Mater. Our principal, Rev. Fr. Gokavi, was a man who was revered by all the teachers, a man who every student looked up to as a role model, a man who was respected by all the parents too.

It was a norm in the school, a practice that had been going on ever since we could remember, that whenever our school wins any inter-school tournament, the next working day would be declared a holiday. Of course, all students welcomed this and looked forward to it, as they would all feel the pride and enjoy the extra day off and would even "dig it in" with friends from other schools.

During the academic year of 1975 we were faced with a horrific war situation between India and Pakistan, and there was a state of Emergency declared. Due to this, we had a hard time studying due to a blackout of power in the evenings, and also had many unforeseen holidays which had us struggling to cover the curriculum. We were close to the end of the year, in the final term, and all teachers needed to engage us with additional special classes being added to cover the subjects in full before the exams.

Our school managed to win a nail-biting-finish cricket tournament. From the jaws of defeat, and with some miracle the team somehow fought back to win. This created a major pandemonium when practically all of us who were watching, just ran out on to the stadium center to celebrate. We could only stop our jubilant expressive demonstration when we heard the start of the award ceremony. This brought us to a silence, and we clapped our way through the prize distribution ritual.

We were all awaiting the announcement of the holiday, the next day, and in particular, I wished for it, as we were due to have a Biology Lab and I was dreading going for it, as our teacher had said that we would be dissecting a frog.

Our Sports Teacher quickly congratulated the players and closed his speech with no mention of the holiday. Soon, we heard loud voices from my schoolmates, all chanting in rhythm – "Holiday, Holiday, We want a holiday" – this went on for about a minute.

The teacher looked helplessly around, as another senior teacher came in and made the same announcement with a lot more firmness in his voice. The same chant repeated and even louder this time – "Holiday, Holiday, We want a holiday."

The matter drew our Vice Principal to come up to speak. He tried to explain and provide all the reasons why such a decision had to be taken. He tried to encourage us by suggesting that we could celebrate together in school and then get to the study routine which we were otherwise lagging behind on. For a moment, the crowd was reflecting on his words and reasons, and then the same chant started all over again, and what started in a small voice soon became a loud chant, and it went on and on. It did not look like it would ever stop until the holiday was declared.

Then, Fr. Gokavi came up with his usual brisk walk, and with the air of authority that somehow exuded from him, he calmly picked up the microphone. His stout figure and his mesmerizing smile got us to pause our chant. We were expecting him to concede. He, in his usual steady voice, first congratulated the players, and then went on to say "I wish I could give you this holiday which is what we deserve, but my priority is that all of you do not lose on your education. Keeping your best interests in mind, I regret that we cannot have a holiday this time."

The stadium went silent. A long one at that.

This time around, not one voice opposed.

It is perhaps easy to brush this aside saying it was a person who had the power or influence based on his position, but what I saw happen (and I was a part of it too) was that all of us actually appreciated him for it, and we were back in school with our full self – body, heart, and mind.

Wow! The influence of a Great Man – Great Leader.

Another small but significant incident that also highlights this point.

I was invited to be a part of a Rotary Club. My proposer Mr. Rao had invited me to attend a meeting before I took the final decision of joining. The cause of service above self, the tagline associated with Rotary was very appealing. What I had heard was that all the members were high achieving leaders from all walks of life, and I was feeling very tentative, as I was in the early stage of my entrepreneurial career. I was feeling very good about being invited into such an organization, where, for many, a membership was very aspirational.

It was a rainy day, with a steady drizzle that was on for quite a long time. I managed to get to the hotel venue where the meeting was to be held, a little earlier than the scheduled time. I nervously walked into the room, looking for Mr. Rao. As I entered, I saw only one person in the room, a fair, well-groomed person in an impeccable custom-made grey suit, in a white shirt and a tie to match. He was trying to set up the projection system, and behind me, two of the hotel staff also walked in, and he was asking them for some help. As he saw me, he turned around and with a warm and friendly smile, he greeted me and extended his hand. He went on to introduce himself, "Good evening, I am Rotarian Raja."

The warmth in his greeting made me feel very comfortable, and I got around to introducing myself and speaking to him. I would have usually retreated and stepped out to wait for Mr. Rao so that I could be introduced to others and perhaps then get around to a conversation. As people came in, he was taking the lead and introducing me to the other members, and it so happened that I also knew a few of them from my earlier business and social associations. Nevertheless, even after a few decades that have gone by, my sense of belonging to the Rotary was triggered by that one incident, which is still so fresh in my mind, that even today I can recall all the details of that day. That evening I saw him lead the meeting, yes, he was the President of the club that year; his humility, his warmth his caring and affection that he showed towards me, especially considering that he was a successful business leader while I was perhaps at a stage at least 20 years behind. To me, even to this day, he is MY PRESIDENT – a leader that could connect with everyone, and I must also admit that there has been great learning for me, by just staying associated with him. There have been many great leaders that followed him at Rotary, and each one has excelled in this dimension of creating that belongingness amongst all the members.

We also still see these ways of working in today's world. You have people build themselves based on the role models that inspire them, learning from them, trying to be like them; to the extent that they copy by getting their hair styling, or the clothes they wear or mimicking the way they walk or talk, in the hope of becoming one like them. They try to see their leader in themselves and boost their confidence that perhaps inspires them. In fact, many popular advertisements and marketing companies exploit this very well even today.

Let's look at the environment where this type of leadership flourished.

At the time when people were looking at the next level, the third layer in the Maslow's Hierarchy of Needs – namely, love and belonging, they were seeking leaders who could connect with them emotionally and provide them that sense of belonging with the leader. Corporates were now getting structured well, options for jobs were a lot more, and skilled workers were available. Markets were opening up, and products were becoming more readily available. What would now attract people was if a leader could establish a deep connection and bond with them through good communication. Thus, communication skills and presentation skills quickly differentiated the successful leaders from the others.

Many leaders were however yet to see this change and wanted to hold on to their authority. Leaders below them were struggling, as they had to deal with the next level of people working. I happened to face two situations that were identical.

First, I was the head of a company and had an executive assistant, let's call her Kala, and this incident is about her. She was very efficient at her work and served her role very well with a lot of dedication and loyalty. She was moderately qualified, as she could not raise the money to continue her higher education, though she had the intellect for it. She made up for this with her commitment and experience. She was working to support her mother and brother, who were both dependent on her income. Financially she was just able to manage with prudent spending around her own needs.

This was an IT company with many different service lines – computer hardware trading, embedded systems, and medical transcription as the core and of course allied lines like training to add to the range of services offered.

She had access to all information about the company, its plans, and strategies, and was more or less driving the day to day administrative work. Every year, she was being recognized not only by me but also by the head of the group of companies, who was also the person financing this venture.

All was going well for the last three years which was all its lifetime as well. The company had been able to get good long-term connects with clients as well. One fine day, or should I say fateful day, I was called in by the board of directors, and was given a single line command – "Get Kala to resign." I was a bit taken aback and could not figure out what was going on. I was still sitting in my chair and was trying to come to terms with the instruction given. My mind was racing to think of what might have happened for this instruction to come, and could not think of any. I went into the probe mode to determine what happened, but all I got was the same line, which was gradually becoming louder with every question I asked. I realized that this was a non-negotiable command.

I was torn between my value system and carrying out a direct instruction from my boss. While I was leaning heavily towards the former, and mentally weighing the pros and cons for Kala, I realized that she would need to be protected, and yet had to get her to resign. I realized that it would be best for me to carry out the command so that her financial settlement could be best handled, and not have this enforced by the board, where they may push for a shortchanged settlement as well. I was also debating in my mind about what would be the impression I would create in enforcing a command without any explanations or reasons. It may have given a wrong impression about me at that time, but I dreaded the consequences that if they had to force their way and actually fire her, she would have probably also faced a financial impact to worry about.

So finally, I had to bite the bullet and get her to resign. A leadership decision on my part to look at the best possible option for a team member.

Soon after this decision, I offered to help find her another job, but she was so hurt that she just completely went off my radar, and even to this day I do not know what she thinks of me. I still believe that in the given situation I did what was most appropriate. However, the guilt behind this made me resign after a short period post this incident.

It was definitely an overpowering of authority in an influence era. I traced back about the company, and it looks like the board of directors had learned that they needed to change their ways of working, which they did, and are now sailing along well, although they may not be the leaders in the industry which were the potential they had. Perhaps with some more changes in leadership ways, they could get back up and challenge some of the current forerunners in their industry.

The second incident, very similar, where I was heading an ITeS company and was hired by a competent HR person, let's call her Rachana. She had hired me with the intent of attempting to turn around this company and close the red situation on their balance sheet, and gradually make the business profitable.

The team in Operations and Sales that I had were a brilliant group of people and had amazing ideas. They all were supportive of me coming in as well, quite contrary to my expectations, as I thought that some of them might be vying for the spot I was hired into. The Directors of the company also were very supportive and gave me a free hand to make the changes that could achieve this goal.

In a short span of four months, the changes started showing results. All of us were in celebration mode and contemplating the next level of growth. We started to prepare for this next leap as well.

Here again, we had the same situation, where I was sent an instruction to fire Rachana, and with no explanations attached to it. This time around, I knew my options, and I went with the same decision as before and got her to step down. I knew that the power equation, if not handled right, would affect her financially and her future career as well. Once again, my team instinct got the better of me and had her exit all cleared and settled. This time around I also resigned soon after and had no hesitation at all. I was clear this time around, that if a leader is being manipulated, then it is not a good situation to be in.

I have not been able to connect again with Rachana, as she continues to nurse a grudge against me, which I understand, but then this is the price a leader sometimes needs to pay if they have to support their team. Through indirect channels, I was happy to know that she has grown in her career to great heights and I am glad that my way of protecting her ensured that she could continue to grow.

The learning for me from these incidents is to be able to build that level of trust amongst your team, where such unexplainable actions also does not affect your relationship, and they trust you to that extent that they believe that whatever you did was in their best interests as well. This level of trust is needed to be able to influence your team positively and get their total support towards you. It is also equally important to build that level of trust upwards so that you get the right answers required for you to lead better. This was perhaps the gap in my leadership capability at that time.

A lot many people started to build these capabilities, as they evolved to leadership positions. It was common for many companies to help their identified future leaders develop these skills of communication.

Gradually, communication and presentation skills were getting ingrained into basic education too. After all, educators are quick to see what is happening in the industry, determine these needs, and quickly integrate it into mainstream education, so that they can create more capable potential leaders.

As many people began to possess basic leadership qualities, people started to compare and identify the better amongst them. This gave rise to other popular theories around being positive, being an authentic leader, and other similar variants of these.

The environment around the markets was all about focus on efficiency and scale. Consumer behavior studies and customer surveys started to gain popularity. Analysis of these was driving the next curve, and analysts were predicting the directional change of products and services, based on customer demands. Organizations were recognizing that customer was king. They were all now looking at CSAT (customer satisfaction) scores to predict their future. Competition analysis and the race to be best CSAT in their important segment was on. In the quest to enhance the game, quality focus, and customer delight became mantras for organizations to grow. The economy was also opening up as consumer buying started to increase.

As the leadership approach of trying to increase efficiency alone was not able to cope with these new analysis findings, the era had to evolve again. New products, better products, and more customer demands were now responsible for moving the leadership approach to look at how to transform their businesses and align their people with this changing need that they were being pushed into. New business strategies were emerging, products and services were getting bundled together to try to be the one-stop point of contact for the customer. Organizations that were only product focused or only service focused had to transform now to manage both together. This took a turn into the next level of evolution of leadership.

Here is a little space for you to capture or reflect upon a story of yours, where you recollect the power and usefulness of an influencer type of leader.

The leader's name:

What were your needs at that time:

The incident:

The Transformational Era.

This era has been around for a long time now. Change Management of different kinds was the focus. Some organizations started to invest in their people being able to get comfortable in extending their comfort zones and managing change. There was a lot of buzz in the various conferences around collaboration, managing mergers, harnessing diversity, and the likes of these depending on different situations that they were facing. During times of change, there are going to be many hard decisions too, and the need to focus on building trust was another dimension that would help in this era to transform and drive growth.

Organizations were starting to morph into a single point of contact for products and services. Acquisitions and mergers started to be the quickest way to integrate offering into the market. The world was starting to change at a rapid rate.

Science and technology were at the forefront of causing this change, and adoption of technology was high and fast. This also aided cost management, as customers were demanding more for less. Product life cycles were getting shorter, and the need to establish the next sigmoid curve was important. The competition was increasing; quality demands were high, policies were aligning to favor customers and consumers. Movement of goods and people across geographies was on the rise. For many of these situations, technology was a key game changer. Skilled workers were increasingly available, and old ones needed reskilling. Communication was easy and instantaneous, and multiple channels were available. Money was a lot easier to come by. More wants started to become needs. The speed of execution and providing of the integrated end to end services was getting more important and highly valued.

With change becoming an integral part, leaders had to adopt ways to deal with the transformation that was needed to match the speed of change. Change Management became a hot topic and one that all organizations were trying to work towards. Companies were picking selective changes and attempting to address them, based on their situations in relation to the markets.

Adoption of technology that seemed easy did begin quite soon. Organizations started investing in and upgrading their machines, deploying robotics, artificial intelligence, and other such tools and inventions. This brought about a leadership challenge on how to upskill their employees to use all of this, and how to map processes that would align with these changes. The question haunting many were, how to address the fears that were in the minds of people who now started feeling insecure. How do we get them to learn new ways of doing things. The people side of things was becoming a big challenge.

There was also a lot of resistance to the change, as people were being moved out of their comfort zones. The ones who could not see the change coming, or could not adapt to them, all wilted. Be it the best people, or even entire organizations. There are lots of examples where organizations missed seeing the paradigm shift coming, and they were forced to shut shop. Leaders had to be adept at change management, and all-around change adoption was what they had to push for.

The ones that got around were the successful leaders of this era – the transformational era.

A medical corollary here probably brings out the dilemma faced by leaders.

When you have a headache setting in, do you seek help from a general physician, or would you go to a specialist, or perhaps even self-medicate? With online information, that could sometimes make you believe that you are facing something very serious, rather than a simple headache, it could scare you and get you to consulting multiple doctors. Similarly, in the corporate sector, on sensing an issue, what would you do, hire a specialist consultant to diagnose, or would you rather use your internal team, or perhaps as a leader take your own course? The kind of reading, or assessments like the engagement pulse, or the 360 feedback that your team could come up with could throw up some options, to help you take a call.

At this stage, there were many theories that would get leaders to be successful. More and more people were building a variety of skills in their quest to lead effectively. Leaders were getting innovative and applying all kinds of measures, and the race was getting hotter. Some styles that became popular include situational leadership, authentic leadership, values-based leadership and many more. Some innovative leaders even blended these approaches based on the situations that they were facing. When speaking to some of the leaders, I would get a standard response – it depends!" and this was starting to get annoying for many – depends on what?

A unique situation of mine is worth mentioning to bring out the kind of creativity that prevailed in this time. This is about transforming a State (name held back intentionally) Youth Association, to enable it to get back to achieving its vision.

This association was formed by a group of 12 philanthropic businessmen who joined hands to support the cause of education for the underprivileged. It was inspired by another group in a different state doing the same thing, and also guided and supported by one of the members there. All the members from a northern region of India that had settled down in Bangalore were excited and drove this cause. These members worked closely together from its inception, and funding the noble cause was done by the members itself, who were contributing to their earnings. Fellowship amongst the members was at its best and the bonding even extended to all the families of these members; all supporting and working together – it was like one large happy family. Soon enough, we also saw the next generation stepping in to strengthen this organization. Seeing the public appeal and success that this movement created, and the need for widening the support to this great cause, and the interest shown by a lot more people to join the movement, they extended membership, and more people joined in. Initially, with this expansion, they furthered the cause and gained amazing popularity, creating high impact in the community. There were many beneficiaries who now went on to hold high positions in the corporate and the government sectors. It was common for members to meet people and when they mentioned that they were from this association, a lot of awe and respect was given to them, and getting their work done in many situations got easier and faster.

Like most organizations as they grew, there came about different schools of thought, different suggestions on how to further the cause, while they were all still aligned to the core vision. Groupism started to emerge. Fellowship started to dwindle. People started to hold back on their purses, and not support the cause as much as they could have, they wanted to drive the "how-to" in their own ways. The fellowship side struggled the most, and this resulted in a steady erosion of their noble work, it is often said that fellowship brings you together to drive the vision. Members just ganged up, and if anyone group proposed something, the other group would shoot it down, irrespective of what was being proposed. This struggle for power soon resulted in people abstaining from taking on a leadership position in this State (withholding the real name for privacy reasons) Youth Association, or when someone actually did take on the mantle, the support was inadequate to deliver to the goals. To make things difficult, no one would talk openly about the situation – no one was prepared to address the elephant in the room.

The Annual General Body meeting where leadership was to be passed on, was becoming difficult. Some past leaders took up the mantle again hoping to revive it but were not successful. Old ways were not working anymore. The democratic structure of a committee steering this ship was becoming difficult as there was this groupism rearing its ugly face now and then, though the mandate was that it should remain democratic.

It was time to do something differently – a transformation was needed.

Finally, I did step in to try something out of the box. An experiment, if you may call it that, to see how some innovative ways could perhaps turn this around in the long run.

The new committee was formed with me being given the mantle to lead, no one else was actually willing to take it up anyway, and the team that I had was chosen such that the representation from different groups were all made part of it.

The burning issue was on how to align people to start supporting financially and by participating in the fellowships and the service events and keep their differences away. Trying to motivate them with the vision was tried too many times before, and failed miserably.

I had a series of meetings with the more experienced people who had their own valid perspectives on how to possibly turn things around. The common thread was on the gaining agreement to raise the funding through the members.

The first change that we were thus attempting was to increase the subscription, which was overdue for the last ten years or so. It was obviously not possible to run the association in current times with funds that account for running it ten years ago.

The established process was that the managing committee for the year would deliberate and make their recommendation to the General Body and seek their approval for such changes. In the past ten years, this was constantly opposed, often with contradicting the reasons for the need to raise the subscription. This time around, we did the computation and got all the data in place to substantiate our request. We were all set to explain to the group and get their approval for the raise. After all, with compelling data, how can anyone refuse. In the managing committee meeting, it was agreed unanimously that we should go for it. I did sense that this was only being said, but was unsure whether they really were supporting it.

I then sought the advice of some senior members, who also agreed with my perceptions, that it would get opposed. One person, in particular, my godfather, and one of the founders gave me one very important piece of advice. He said, "people need a forum to vent and oppose completely so that they can feel that they have won. Once their ego is satisfied, there is a possibility that things could change."

These words were constantly nagging me, and as I was contemplating the actions, an idea dawned on me. This idea though meant that I would have to take up the bigger cause as my focus, and be prepared to lose a smaller battle, and allow others to win. The cause of education was so dear to me that I found the courage needed to go for it, take on this experiment, and risk my otherwise neutral image in the group.

Finally, the day of the General Body meeting arrived. It was planned for the General Body Meeting, to be held at the Local Cricket Association, to keep the costs down to the minimum. It was a bright sunny Sunday afternoon, and members started coming in. One could sense the tension in the air, and though members were smiling and holding friendly conversations while waiting for the meeting to start, it was evident that this was just a mask hiding their real emotions. The short sentences with which people were speaking was a clear indicator.

The meeting was called to order, and the pin drop silence that followed was nerve-racking. The anxiety could be felt in the heaviness of the atmosphere in the room.

Very intentionally, many reforms were being tabled, and one by one, all of them were being opposed citing some frivolous reasons. It was very clear that the mood was to oppose every change that was being put on the table, in particular, the focus was on the fee increase that was to be targeted to be shot down.

When we came to the core agenda, the increase in the subscription, I took a long pause, trying to gauge what people may be anticipating, and also allowing people to focus their thoughts. They were anticipating that I would read out the circulated piece of information and ask the members to recommend any other options they may have before putting this up to vote. Instead, and to everyone's surprise, I directly called for it to be voted, and of course, it was opposed and opposed with a large margin.

At that moment, many felt victorious. Some of the members who were a little concerned about this showed their sympathy, citing that this should not have been opposed and there were few that also called out that it was a strategic mistake to not look for a partial increase option that could have been accepted. While I heard them, and played along with the emotional feel around, inside me, I felt happy. I was playing for the war and not the little battle, the words of my godfather, and the goal of the bigger cause was very clear for me. While I maintained my calm and did not respond to any of the views floating around on that day, it certainly was hard for me to stand by the fact that a good well researched and the documented appeal was rejected. As they say – you need to pick the battles you fight, and pick the ones you are willing to lose, so that finally you win the war. I was hoping that this strategic move would help the association in the long run.

And, that was exactly how it turned out. Two years later, the new committee tabled the same request and even adapted to the new needs that were a little higher, and this got approved without any resistance. I had that new leader come to me, and thank me for the courage shown in losing out earlier, to smoothen the path for the future. I guess he could see through the strategy. As it stands today, it makes me feel proud to see this organization is continually growing from strength to strength, and increase the level of service to the community multifold. This year they even surpassed all the earlier highs and have been able to touch over 6000 students, again all supported by the funds contributed by its own members. The glory was not fully back, and the transformation is very visible.

What I learned there, was that leadership is a long-term game, and you need to know what you are after. You need to know who is with you, how you keep them with you; you need to know who is not aligned with you, and you use the best possible ways to align them as quickly as you can. You do all this without worrying about what people think of you in the short term, or even perhaps in the longer term, as a leader the real question was about how you can get the maximum number of people to support the cause you are after.

This is one example of a creative adaptation of a leadership approach that worked. It could have failed too. Leaders were doing what they felt suitable and what they were comfortable with. What worked for some didn't work for others, and it was also about the situation prevalent.

This was a time when corporates were starting to focus on results, people were tweaking processes as needed, planning roles within teams that were adapting to external needs, and starting to look at how leaders could not only get results from their teams in various situations but also how they can create other leaders in their teams, while driving their results. Defining the skills of a leader was starting to blur, as there was no possibility of defining "one" way in which you could be sure of being a successful leader.

Meanwhile, the corporate roles were getting structured to focus on results. The HR group was given an increased focus on Leadership Development, Succession planning, and similarly related areas. The different HR personnel looked at various existing approaches and tried to select some options that they could adopt which would possibly work in their situation. Depending on what they chose, and how people tried to use them, they got varying results. A lot of thought was going around on what could be done, or where they could do better, and many forums were discussing success stories and challenges faced.

The call amongst the corporates, when they realized that they had to change the ways of working, people were redefining processes, and attempting transformation of culture to suit the needs driven by the external environment. Lots of emphasis on corporate culture, team culture, aligning values of every individual to those of the company was being attempted. Lots of training interventions and ways of making learning stick was being tried.

Another very good attempt, was defining the ability of a leader to provide clarity of where they were going, set the climate in the team, and have the right competence brought in or built into the team, was gaining popularity, as it was getting results. From this modus operandi, we even saw a framework called Organization Leadership Architecture getting built – an outcome of a lot of research as well.

When we look at the next turn or the next era, leaders were finding it difficult to provide clarity as the world was changing even faster, they were struggling to establish a conducive climate as the members of the team were also changing rapidly, and finding it close to impossible on the competence part, as the multi-generation workforce were not ready to invest in their competence building with the enthusiasm of a constant learner being the core need for this.

The era was changing.

Let's look at the next chapter, where we discuss all the things that were changing and what was the impact of it, which in the next chapter would meaningfully lead to how leaders could now deal with this and find a way forward to lead successfully in this new era.

SANJAY DUGAR

2
WHAT IS THE CHANGE IN THE ENVIRONMENT TODAY?

Most of us have probably heard about VUCA, a term created by Warren Bennis and Burt Nanus, which as an acronym is trying to define the environment today, and is especially important, as a leader, to understand this in a little detail.

Various books, research articles, and blogs discuss this. It has become a hot topic in conferences and learning forums. Everyone seems to be talking about it, but very few talk about how leaders should deal with it. Even if we can take one at a time, we can perhaps find some ways out, but with all four of them playing together, there should be a new way to deal with it. First, let's discuss the four parts in this chapter, and then we can look at ways forward in the next one.

Volatility:

The challenge here is that the situation around creates things which are unexpected or unstable. Even the duration is unpredictable. It may not be hard to understand volatility, as knowledge around it is usually easy to get or acquire. For example, new things emerge with a new player (company), especially a small one, that disrupts the way we work, or price changes that happen after a natural disaster, sanctions that occur between two countries affect the other countries as well, and the list is endless. Knowledge may be available, but can we know what parts of this knowledge is needed and should be considered? This knowledge can throw our planning completely off.

Some suggestions that I have heard or read about is, that one can build slack and increase the workforce to deal with preparation for the unexpected. This has been tried too, and the costs associated with it are very high, and in the age of wafer-thin margins, it can become difficult, and often threaten to push companies into the red. Another suggestion in dealing with this situation, is to look at integrating temporary staffing with the regular ones on a need basis, and this then poses a challenge of variable costing which again threatens the margins for companies to make this viable. The supply chain optimization is another route in dealing with volatility and working with the famous just in time model, thereby minimizing inventory holding costs and optimizing based on customer needs, but, with speed of delivery becoming crucial this option opens up other related risks too.

Holding team members staying on course is difficult and also very demotivating for team members to see their processes change very often. People get frustrated by the change, and change management concepts get fully tested and stretched.

Uncertainty:

The difficulty faced on this element is that while there is inadequate information, the cause and effect are clearly visible. This pushes the case for a change, which is possible but not always acceptable to everyone. It is again not hard to understand uncertainty, as it is seen and felt everywhere. The degree of its impact is perhaps not clear, and hence resistance to change is expected. For example, a competitor comes up with another substitute or even a similar product; it confuses the future of the product or service in the market and for your organization. Or, news articles around research, or social cause movements promoting some merits or showcasing some demerits, can completely derail strategies and plans.

Some suggestions that when deployed has shown some benefits include, investing in information and research, working with data analyses, to interpret and share them; and this combined with suitable organizational structural change to create groups that can provide analytics support, could help reduce uncertainty to some extent. Will that be economically viable, maybe a question.

When strategies and plans change frequently, it makes leading members of such a team very difficult. People start to doubt whether the leader knows what he or she is doing or even aspiring for. It can shake the core foundation of trust, that leaders are constantly trying to build and maintain.

Complexity:

The worry here for leaders is that there are too many moving parts in the game, too many things are interconnected, far too many nested loops of "if ... then or else ...". This makes it difficult to understand and even more difficult to explain. It becomes a very overwhelming task to process, digest, and find ways to move forward. A simple, commonplace example is when a company is operating multi-geography, each having its own unique rules, wide variation in regulations, different tariffs, multiple kinds of tax structures, operating environments, and different cultural values. Knowledge may be available to deal with all of these but would need to be brought together to find excellent ways of working, else it would result in a lot of confusion.

Many experienced consultants usually advise that in order to deal with this situation, one would need to restructure and develop specialists in these areas or even hire them to the level required to unravel the mysteries of these complexities.

When team members are unclear about the ways of working, or feel unsure about it being the right approach, a lot of grapevine views come in, that further complicate the situation. These unreal views confuse people, and it becomes a downward spiral going from bad to worse. For leaders to arrest this feeling, and keep people focused is tough, and one needs to find different ways to lead the team.

Ambiguity:

This is all about the "unknowns." There are absolutely no precedents or indicators that can help provide some information that could help. A good example of this which we can see around us; companies entering into new geographies which are very different from the home market or markets where they have some experience, or when companies choose to add products or services which erstwhile would be considered outside their core capabilities. Acquisitions and mergers often are attempted too in the hope that it bridges some of these gaps, and these come with a whole additional set of challenges.

To overcome this kind of a challenge, companies have attempted experimental pilots, gathered learning, shared successes, and then attempted to scale. This could be one of the means to deal with it; however, the time taken to experiment and get ahead is so large, that the situation would have changed again. Hence, the same way of going about may not yield predictable results. Very often this element of ambiguity has resulted in leaders taking their calculated risks, which sometimes work and sometimes fail. It is unlikely that any leader would see continuous success in a series of situations before them. When team members see a mixed story of successes and failures, they start to think about whether the environment is safe for them, and should they follow this leader. If a leader is to be successful, he or she would need to be very lucky that all their calculated risk-taking working well. Can leadership then be a chance, or. can we find a new way to lead?

As detailed above, each element in itself makes it hard to be a successful leader, and the world is operating with all four of them continually throwing challenges simultaneously. In the simultaneous existence of all the four elements of VUCA, the compounding effect of the problem is very clearly saying that the ways of leading in the past cannot really succeed now or in the future..

The cause of VUCA is perhaps attributed to the extensive research bringing amazing discoveries that change the way we work. We have rapid technological changes that are being lapped up by organizations, and individuals. Further, knowledge is easily accessible, thanks to the internet powered information age that we are in, all of it at our fingertips, literally fingertips with use of smart mobile phones becoming so popular. This increased access to knowledge continues to contribute to increasing needs by consumers, all demanding new innovative products and services, that also need to adapt to the growing lifestyle demands, opening up of globalization, besides many other such factors. VUCA is here to stay and stay for long, maybe forever. It would also be reasonable to expect that VUCA would further accelerate.

Technology is gearing up and starting to gain rapid adoption. Many are scared that automation may take away their jobs. Some are worried that their skills do not match up to these new ways of working. A fear that seniority and experience is not an advantage anymore, and even perhaps having a negative impact. People have started to adjust to these new lifestyles and have committed to large EMIs and are now worried and unsure about their future. Will they be able to survive is now a question they are asking themselves.

The ability of leaders to not only communicate but demonstrate in action, that they care for the employees, the customers, and believe in the vision is of utmost importance. Motivating people is now based on a mix of all of these. Leadership behaviors are being closely watched, to see whether they live up to their messages, their values, and the decisions that are being made. It still is very top down in its outlook, as interpreted by the team they were leading, and they are unsure of the leaders sensing their "real" concerns.

The challenge is clearly here for leaders to find ways to get their teams to whole-heartedly rally behind them. To further add to the confusion, we have a multi-generation workforce that thinks differently, a multicultural workforce that has different values, and amongst dealing with all of these, leaders are not only expected to lead but also build leaders for the future. Leadership has to now deal with various situations that are very individualistic, and one single overarching style is not likely to appeal to everyone. One size does not and cannot fit all. Leadership has to be tweaked to suit multiple situations, and yet convey one clear direction to all. While they are challenged to lead, they also need to ensure that succession plans for future leaders are in place, and nurtured for the future. What then would be the skills that a leader would need to have and use effectively to be able to manage all these demands on them.

A clear case for a new era – **the facilitator era,** is discussed in the next chapter.

3
WHAT WOULD BE A MORE SUITABLE METHOD OF LEADING TODAY?

In the Personality era, it was all about the individual leader and his vision, plans, and direction. A clear autocratic style that drove success. Corporates having such leaders automatically did well and grew. They also created leaders like them as they started to scale. The success story revolved around optimization – call it efficiency, or effectiveness, and a measure of success largely depended on how employees aligned with the leader's directions. It was all about the heart being aligned with the leader's views, and the mind followed directions given. At this time, especially towards the end of this era, even the education system was getting aligned to building personality and integrate this into their curriculum. It was also common for people to attend personality development classes, or finishing schools, in their quest to become successful leaders.

In the Influence era, things changed considerably. Leaders had to connect with the people and also have a logical story that would get people's minds connected too. They needed to inspire masses, and communication was thus the key tool. In this era, success largely depended on how people could see their role in the big picture of the organization. It became important for people to know that how what they did was connected to growth and success. Simon Sinek's Golden Circle (a Ted Talk) showcased this concept in a very simple way to communicate that would appeal to the masses – the why – how – what format. Here again, the education system was getting aligned to this, and communication and presentations skills were getting integrated with their ways of working. It was expected of all students to be able to present their findings or project work; and also a huge recognition for extra-curricular around debate competitions. Having these kinds of extra-curricular achievements on your resume got you the recognition and established a differentiator for you to be able to get an opportunity to be a leader.

In the Transformational era, things changed even faster. For leaders to be successful, they needed to drive significant changes to align with the market demands. This was the time when people were needed to go beyond. They had to be moved out of their comfort zone and yet stay aligned to the leader's call. It was a time when leaders were pushing for their teams to get comfortable with cultural diversity, integrated offerings, cross geography ways of working, mergers with organizations that had a different product or service line, automation, new skill development to stay relevant, and this list could go on and on. Leaders were expected to work with people of different styles and be able to align them all to work together, they had to lead by example, and leadership was tested on how comfortable they were when they were outside their comfort zone too. Teamwork and diversity were what leaders were expected to harness; and hence there was a huge rush amongst organizations seeking to build mastery around skills like high performing teams, team building, leveraging diversity, cross-cultural competence, and other such methods. The academic space also caught up with this need, and it was common for people to be part of schools where cross-cultural groups were your schoolmates, the way projects were run involved working in teams and with diversity included in it, so as to prepare for the leadership journey ahead, or at least to lay a foundation for stretching their comfort zone. Sports was suddenly gaining recognition in the workplace as the ability to lead, work in teams, accept challenges were all qualities that were valued in organizations.

And now, ...

We are at a situation where all these leadership methods that worked earlier in the situations that were prevalent then, and the education system has also caught up with them, today's leaders need something more.

Today, the workforce is a lot smarter; they know what they are good at and what they enjoy. A great definition of using your strengths by Marcus Buckingham has got everyone thinking – strengths are what you are good at AND what you enjoy doing. With customers demanding speed and the forever changing needs that they demand, leaders barely have time to focus on all skills needed; they would find it easier to create teams that would have its members complement one another and together have all the needed skills. It is also the age of agile, where people come together to work on a project, and once done they move on to another project often with another leader as well. The workforce is getting comfortable working this way. The concept is moving towards focusing on strengths and using them as often as possible at work. This also makes the work enjoyable, so that work-life balance is no longer a concern; instead, it is work being life; and when people enjoy what they do, they are motivated to perform at their optimum levels.

Another important thing to note is that information is available easily and is accessible everywhere. The current workforce is adept at getting information quickly and efficiently. Gone are the days, where we would listen to information handed down and try to make sense of it, today people get the information they want in a way they can deal with it too. Reverse mentoring has become an important concept that works to orient the more experienced members on new ways of doing things. To be able to learn from others in the team, regardless of experience, background, and other such things have become the need of the hour. How long can we keep learning from others and on how many different areas? We need to keep learning, is what one would argue. How much time do we have to keep learning then? Would it not be easier to find a way to tap into the knowledge that exists amongst the team members itself.

The concept of harnessing diversity has gone beyond gender and culture. Earlier it was about understanding and appreciating diversity so that one could be a good team and even collaborate amongst teams. That stage has also been moving ahead, it is now also about what do we know about the related things in the area of work, how other perspectives and ideas impact the goal or could significantly change the goal. The demand for INNOVATION is now very significant and has to be addressed. All organizations have this embedded a message in their communication – Innovate or Perish. With perish not being an option, this is a rhetorical statement, clearly saying that innovation is the only way to survive.

Thus, bringing together a variety of information available within the team, which when brought together in the right way, could provide new perspectives, that could foster innovation.

Design thinking concepts are becoming popular, why? It allows for bringing in diverse thinking initially, and then as you work the next steps it converges into an acceptable creative solution that could drive creativity and innovation. Not surprising, why design thinking expertise is sought after by leaders, or even try and build it into their skills.

In the current VUCA world, setting goals or vision is no longer a single person's task, it has become a collective and democratic way of doing it. The need is to see what everyone thinks, and how everyone feels about the vision, mission, goals and how it stays aligned with the overall purpose of the organization. There have been situations where the overall direction of the company has changed too. We have many examples of companies that were leaders in the field and needed a change in direction to survive. Blackberry, Nokia are some great examples of these.

There have been acquisitions and mergers, which have changed the game considerably for them or their competitors, and mergers are becoming increasingly common.

Leaders, those who are to be successful in the future, would need to have the skills to deal with divergence and convergence – that is, bring together diverse perspectives on the table, get the silent ones to talk, and get the talkative ones to listen. The leader should ideally bring forth the emotional situation that the group members would face in implementing a decision. To be able to adapt to the changes that happen, the leaders should be able to get a buy-in from all members of the team. The leader should be able to connect with everyone at the level of self-esteem and actualization. Design thinking being one which showcases this very well. Beyond innovating to serve the market needs, it is also important to keep the team motivated and inspired. The two highest levels of Maslow's Hierarchy of Needs is where the team members are operating in – esteem and self-actualization. What this implies is that everyone today needs to know that his or her knowledge and inputs are valuable, they need to know how their role and their capabilities support the organization in its journey to success. A leader needs to be able to hold meetings where everyone feels engaged and finds that they contribute. It is no longer a top-down, nor is it bottom-up; it is about "altogether." It is not about diversity and decision making; it is about divergence and convergence – it is about acceptance by all, which is only possible by effective conflict management – encouraging conflict in divergence, and managing it in convergence. Leaders that can use group processes to get the teams to share and agree, would be the ones who can lead teams to great outcomes. They are the leaders who would be the ones that organizations are going to depend on, to get them to go where they want to. They are the ones who will align people with their business strategy.

In the many organizations that I work with, it is interesting to see that a few of them, the early adopters, have already started investing in these capabilities, and to me, it is a clear indicator of their future success. It is the way forward. It would be interesting to see how the educators would notice this and start to adopt and teach some of these skills to prepare leaders for the future.

In the next part, we will discuss these skills, a few tools, tips, and techniques, and also possible uses of these skills. Go ahead and enjoy the next part, and prepare yourself to be a successful leader.

PART TWO: SOUNDS LIKE THE COMPETENCIES OF A FACILITATOR

External and internal demands drive leaders today. They need to manage both these push forces constantly.

Externally:

Markets are demanding innovation; they want to see new and more convenient options that would meet and even surpass their needs. Their own needs keep changing, and hence the need to forge partnerships with customers has become the way to move ahead.

Markets are demanding high speed. With new products and services continuously being released in the market, speed plays a crucial role. There is no time for anyone to allow for slow updates in their supply chain, as this would mean market adoption would shift to players who have what they need and acquire them rather than wait for their existing supply chain team to come up with what they need. They would much rather get what they need now as they are unsure too about how long that need will stay.

The shift from quality focus to speed focus is the trend. Of course, a base level of quality is expected. It is thus not surprising that people release products and services, and continue to have a team continually updating or adding more features as they go. It is also, therefore, an excellent opportunity for startups that can operate at the required speed, come up with innovations that threaten to bust the existing companies that cannot operate in this environmental push for speed. Startups and small companies have the advantage of adopting change a lot faster. It is hence not surprising to see the steep rise in the number of startups and also seeing many of them become successful. It is also increasingly common to see startups setting themselves up for acquisitions that can support the scale-up of their operations. Earlier one could wait to get to a certain level, and then gradually scale; but in the VUCA world, there is no time for gradual growth, it has to be quick to reach out to the masses, as over time new players could topple their portfolio significantly.

Internally:

Leaders today need to be able to harness the diverse knowledge in their teams, get everyone to share information openly, and jointly arrive at decisions that are acceptable to the team. They need to foster explicit collaborative partnerships, respect individual perspectives, and let the group commit to tasks that they are willing to deliver on; and ensure that they stay on track. Leaders need to help the team create the environment and decide on the ways of working that would be optimum to achieve the goals.

Leaders cannot afford to be biased, based on the information they have, as the collective group would most likely have a lot more information; cannot be biased based on their experiences of the past, as the world in the current time would have moved significantly forward and the old ways cannot be possibly the best new ways, and it would be with the help of the group that they would have to find the way ahead that would work best, including how often they need to group up to review whether their planned objectives and goals are still relevant.

When changes happen at this speed, it is but natural for people to feel frustrated and even demotivated. Stress levels would continue to soar. The group decisions in most cases are likely to be with incomplete information. To be able to keep the group on course would mean a constant exchange of information very transparently. The fact that people are now looking at the top two layers of the Maslow's hierarchy, namely, esteem and self-actualization will also be another important aspect which will push leaders to facilitate. They would always have to strive to have everyone aligned. To add to this, teams are seeking convenient work timings, and work locations too, which makes this an even harder challenge to cope with.

Being aware that in the interactions with their teams, are there any "sounds of silence," and should they do something to get all the inputs out on the table, is something that can set the successful leader apart from the rest of the pack. The leadership methods are moving from a "tell" to an "ask" mode.

When we look at the competencies of a leader in this environment and match it to the ones of a facilitator, you see that they are almost the same. In the next chapter, this is discussed in more detail.

SANJAY DUGAR

4
THE COMPETENCIES REQUIRED OF A LEADER, MATCHES THAT OF A FACILITATOR

The leader of today has to drive meetings skillfully, all kinds of meetings, strategy formulation meetings, employee meetings, team meetings, cross-functional team meetings, project meetings, stakeholder meetings, task force meetings, goal setting meetings, and this list could be endless. The meetings would also serve different objectives and purposes. With speed being a major consideration in today's VUCA environment, it is important to have these meetings run effectively. It is common knowledge that many corporate employees spend significant time in meetings that do not get to achieve their purpose. A lot of time and money is spent, besides the frustration and agony that it causes amongst them.

How many meetings have we led or attended where we have been disappointed with the time invested? How many meetings have we, in retrospect, felt later that the meeting was not as productive as expected? Well, we are not alone in this, research shows that $37 billion per year is spent on unsuccessful meetings, 37% of productive time is spent in meetings, 60 meetings per month is the average, over 70% bring other work into meetings, AND, people feel more exhausted when attending meetings and perceive that they have a higher workload.

Let me share an incident that may highlight this.

The cricket team that I was leading, had just lost the 3rd consecutive match in the league games. We were the marked favorites, and hence losing even one game was not expected. Needless to mention, the team was demotivated. We decided that we need to have a two-day outing and regroup ourselves to build a stronger team bonding amongst us. We were hoping that this would help turn things around. To plan this two-day trip, we decided that we would meet over dinner and make our plans.

Rahul, jumped in quickly to say that he would arrange the venue, and we all knew that he would be the best at it, as he was a foodie, and so we all agreed. Just about two hours later, he had finalized the date, time, and venue for our dinner meeting and made the necessary bookings that were needed, considering that Friday evening was the best option for us, and that meant that all restaurants would be crowded.

He had selected a place in the central area so that it would be convenient for everyone to reach there. The table booked for us was the outdoor area, under a huge banyan tree, and a little isolated from the other smaller clusters that were there too. It was the perfect setting that would enable us to hold our conversations without disturbing the neighboring diners. While the time set was 7.30pm, we were all there by 7.15 pm itself, all excited to work out our plans. 18 out of the 20 of us were present; two could not come as they had some other commitments.

Though the hangover of the 3 consecutive losses were having our spirits dampened a bit, however, being under the green cover of a huge banyan tree, a nice big and very elegantly set up round table that could seat us all, the dim lights with a yellow tint, the soothing background instrumental music, did manage to raise our spirits to some extent. Added to it, perhaps the agenda was exciting enough for us to be wholeheartedly present in the meeting.

After the initial greetings and everyone settling down in their chairs, we saw a stout, short man briskly walking up to our table, and he with exaggerated politeness introduced himself to us as the manager. He went on to say that the food order was preset for us as decided by Rahul at the time of the booking itself. He then with a wave of his hand, indicated for two waiters to come over, and asked them to take care of the needs on our table. So with that out of the way too, we started on our agenda.

All eyes were turned towards me, and I took the lead. After the brief background, as a build-up from our earlier discussions, we had finalized that we would go next Saturday and return on Sunday. I mentioned that we needed to pick a place that would enable us to be together doing something as a team and that as we would also do an overnight stay, we could also think of something for the evening. There was silence, and it felt like everyone was waiting to hear my next thought. After a slightly awkward silence, and to get things started on the venue, I decided that I would throw in an initial option and see how others would respond. I suggested a resort located about an hour's drive away from the city center, with the intent of starting deliberations around what others think about it, and hoping for some other options too. I also did have some other better options in my mind, well, at least better options from my perspective; and as we went around the table, everyone was supporting this first option. We got everyone nodding and saying something to the effect of giving their consent to it. Now, I was reluctant to share my other option, as it was obvious that everyone in the group was in approval of this one.

We went ahead with making the arrangements for all of us to go there. We even negotiated a sharing basis of 4 in a room, going by the large room size that could accommodate extra beds. All 20 of us would go together on a small bus so that we also travel together.

We set out after breakfast, at about 10.30am. The expected one hour drive, took us a little over that, and we got in around noon, which was okay since our check in time was noon anyway. As we entered the resort, we were shocked to see the entire lawn area littered and not cleaned up. We could see some of the staff working towards tidying it up though. We then approached the reception area to check in, and we were told that there would be a delay by about 2 hours, since last night they were catering to a big party, and today they were understaffed. We decided to have lunch while we were waiting, and the lunch was also very disappointing, It felt like the buffet had leftovers brought out. To add to our woes, our rooms were also not cleaned properly, and many of us were struggling to get the extra towels needed, as we were four to a room, instead of the customary two. With all these happening, we found it hard to stay focused on some activities planned, and all in all, the trip was a total let down.

As we were returning in the bus on Sunday late afternoon, I was seated next to Suraj, and he mumbled, "I knew it, we should have chosen another place." Listening to him, and having gone through this unpleasant experience myself too, I asked him in a very tentative voice, "Suraj, did you have any other suggestions in mind?" and without waiting for a response, added another question, "Why did you not bring it up during our meeting, as you were also there?" His instant response was, "I thought everyone else was happy with this option, so why change and cause more unwanted discussions."

As I started discussing this individually with the others, what came up was that none of them wanted to go to this resort, not even me. No one spoke up, as they felt that it would create time-consuming discussions and could even cause some contradictions or conflicts, while we were trying to rebuild the team bond.

That was when I realized that my leadership failed, as I was unable to sense and manage the Abilene Paradox that took over the discussions.

The Abilene Paradox is a situation that many leaders get into; it is a situation in which the group decides on a course of action that is counter to the preferences of any of the individuals in the group.

One could argue, that the individuals are to be blamed for this failure and not so much the leader alone, as they all withheld their point of view. What I would say is, it is up to the leader to be able to ask himself or herself, "what is my role in the problem?" and then go about resolving it. In all failures, it can only be the leader who is responsible.

It could be the culture within the team, or it could be the facilitation process and style used; whichever it be, this could be overcome with good facilitation practices by a leader.

Many of us have probably faced similar things in our work.

I have heard from senior leaders about how their high stakes meetings have also gone in the wrong direction, as the leader failed to manage the Abilene Paradox. There have been instances where multi-million dollars have been lost because of this.

This is just one kind of meeting – where the Sounds of Silence could not be heard by the leader. When critical information is not brought out, a meeting will fail. Other kinds of meetings go through the same kind of problem, and it is definitely, the facilitation skill of the leader that could ensure that this does not happen.

Let's look at some of the desired outcomes in meetings that a leader would face in the VUCA world.

1. Understanding Market Trends

Leaders today need to access information about what is happening in the marketplace that directly and indirectly affect their portfolio. For this, they would need to keep in touch with the latest research and technology, all of which is advancing at a rapid speed. They will need to analyze these developments and creatively think of how this could impact them. They will also need to be able to predict the next set of changes.

The ability to get everyone to share the information they have, and then to get their opinion on the information would be a critical skill.

2. Eliciting Customer Needs

Leaders would have to constantly stay in touch with their customers and keep track of their business strategy. They would need to elicit information from customers on their current and future needs. They would also have to be able to showcase their expertise in shaping the future of their customers business, aligned with their strategy.

This specific capability of a leader matches the role of Business Analyst, who in their quest to gather requirements use a variety of facilitation tools and techniques.

The ability to elicit information and set expectations aligned to their business strategy would be a critical skill.

3. Dealing with Ambiguity

Leaders would often not have enough time or the reach to get all the information they need to make informed decisions, as everything is changing too fast and often not clear. In this situation, and with the pressure of speed, they will need to make decisions and take risks associated with ambiguity.

The ability to make decisions in consensus without all the information available, and setting expectations with the team that the decisions may change would be a critical skill.

4. Fostering Collaboration

Based on the above two competencies, they would need to look at opportunities from research and technology that favor them, and find ways to establish partnerships; and where they sense threats, they would need to find countermeasures to stay ahead in the game.

The ability to find common ground to have external stakeholders support their team would be a critical skill.

5. Driving Innovation

To be able to innovate constantly, they would need to establish a culture where teams are created with a lot of diversity, diversity of all kinds – culture, background, interests, hobbies, gender, geographies, age, and many more. They will need to establish ways of communicating not only within teams but also with multiple teams. This would be further complicated as communication needs, and medium would be different amongst the members of diverse team composition.

The ability to work with the team to define the culture that would work in the best interests of all to deliver their work, and support one another; establish the environment where teams can experiment without fear, and share the outcomes without feeling scared, would be a critical skill.

6. Conflict Management

While harnessing diversity for its advantages, it certainly would raise many and frequent conflicts. These conflicts would be needed to generate multiple advantages, often providing direction for the short term ahead, and would need to be managed well, to be able to keep the team continuing to work together and achieve their tasks on time.

The ability to first bring the conflict into the open, and then to have them successfully resolved where everyone feels heard and come to an agreement on ways forward, would be a critical skill.

7. Change Management

To deal with the constant changes that are bound to happen in this situation, managing the process of change would be a continuous need, and leaders would have to be adept at it. Further, they would need to be able to adopt change themselves.

The ability to showcase their comfort with change, and then helping others in the team on willingly and successfully go through their change journey, so that they can adapt, adopt, and become adept in what they need to do, would be a critical skill.

The impact of VUCA, with the requirements from the external and internal stakeholders, and the expectations of a leader, some good facilitation practices, that would help a leader tide over these situations is essential.

A "facilitator" is a guide or "discussion leader" for the group. The process of facilitation is a way of providing leadership without taking the reigns. A facilitator's job is to get others to assume responsibility and take the lead. The definition of facilitating is "to make easy" or "ease a process." What a facilitator does is the plan, guide and manage a group event to ensure that the group's objectives are met effectively, with clear thinking, good participation and full buy-in from everyone who is involved.

Facilitation is a way of providing leadership to a group by managing the process for the group to arrive at the outcome. For example, a team leader offering team members a method with which they can develop their ways out to resolve a problem, or to find their next steps. In this case, the leader is not suggesting the how or what to do, instead of letting the group find their way, and at the same time, the group is not feeling abandoned as the leader is guiding them through the process in a methodical manner so that the group arrives at the steps forward.

While looking at the competencies of a leader today, it is, therefore, essential to include facilitation skills. Further, as the practice of facilitation is also evolving at high speed, with more methods and tools getting created and use, the need to constantly upskill on this is also equally essential for a leader to be able to deal with the current changing environment and continue to drive the organization towards its goals successfully.

Let's then look at what are the skills of a competent

facilitator, and for that, we shall use the Core Competencies defined by the International Association of Facilitators (IAF). The IAF has published this in their website, that allows you to download them too – https://www.iaf-world.org/site/professional/core-competencies. This list is provided here, and one can easily see the similarity in skills needed to be a successful leader matches that of a competent facilitator.

The Core Competencies of a Facilitator.

A. Create Collaborative Client Relationships

A1. Develop working partnerships

- Clarify mutual commitment
- Develop consensus on tasks, deliverables, roles & responsibilities
- Demonstrate collaborative values and processes such as in co-facilitation

A2. Design and customize applications to meet client needs

- Analyse organizational environment
- Diagnose client need
- Create appropriate designs to achieve intended outcomes
- Predefine a quality product & outcomes with client

A3. Manage multi-session events effectively

- Contract with a client for scope and deliverables
- Develop event plan
- Deliver event successfully
- Assess or evaluate client satisfaction at all stages of the event or project

B. Plan Appropriate Group Processes

B1. Select clear methods and processes that:

- Foster open participation with respect for client culture, norms, and participant diversity
- Engage the participation of those with varied learning or thinking styles
- Achieve a high-quality product or outcome that meets the client needs

B2. Prepare time and space to support group process

- Arrange physical space to support the purpose of the meeting
- Plan effective use of time
- Provide effective atmosphere and drama for sessions

C. Create and Sustain a Participatory Environment

C1. Demonstrate effective participatory and interpersonal communication skills

- Apply a variety of participatory processes
- Demonstrate effective verbal communication skills
- Develop rapport with participants
- Practice active listening
- Demonstrate the ability to observe and provide feedback to participants

C2. Honor and recognize diversity, ensuring inclusiveness
- Encourage positive regard for the experience and perception of all participants
- Create a climate of safety and trust
- Create opportunities for participants to benefit from the diversity of the group
- Cultivate cultural awareness and sensitivity

C3. Manage group conflict

- Help individuals identify and review underlying assumptions
- Recognise conflict and its role within group learning/maturity
- Provide a safe environment for conflict to surface
- Manage disruptive group behavior
- Support the group through a resolution of conflict

C4. Evoke group creativity

- Draw out participants of all learning/thinking

styles
- Encourage creative thinking
- Accept all ideas
- Use approaches that best-fit needs and abilities of the group
- Stimulate and tap group energy

D. Guide Group to Appropriate and Useful Outcomes

D1. Guide the group with clear methods and processes

- Establish a clear context for the session
- Actively listen, question and summarize to elicit the sense of the group
- Recognize tangents and redirect to the task
- Manage small and large group process

D2. Facilitate group self-awareness about its task

- Vary the pace of activities according to the needs of the group
- Identify information the group needs, and draw out data and insight from the group
- Help the group synthesize patterns, trends, causes, frameworks for action
- Assist the group in reflection on its experience

D3. Guide the group to consensus and desired outcomes

- Use a variety of approaches to achieve group consensus
- Use a variety of approaches to meet group objectives
- Adapt processes to changing situations and needs of the group
- Assess and communicate group progress
- Foster task completion

E. Build and Maintain Professional Knowledge

E1. Maintain a base of knowledge

- Be knowledgeable in management, organizational systems and development, group development, psychology, and conflict resolution
- Understand the dynamics of change
- Understand learning/ thinking theory

E2. Know a range of facilitation methods

- Understand problem-solving and decision-making models
- Understand a variety of group methods and techniques
- Know the consequences of misuse of group methods
- Distinguish process from task and content
- Learn new processes, methods, & models in support of client's changing/emerging needs

E3. Maintain professional standing

- Engage in ongoing study/learning related to our field
- Continuously gain awareness of new information in our profession
- Practice reflection and learning
- Build personal industry knowledge and networks
- Maintain certification

F. Model Positive Professional Attitude

F1. Practice self-assessment and self-awareness

- Reflect on behavior and results
- Maintain congruence between actions and personal and professional values
- Modify personal behavior/style to reflect the needs of the group
- Cultivate an understanding of one's values and their potential impact on work with clients

F2. Act with integrity

- Demonstrate a belief in the group and its possibilities
- Approach situations with authenticity and a positive attitude
- Describe situations as the facilitator sees them and inquire into different views
- Model professional boundaries and ethics (as described in the IAF's Statement of Values and Code of Ethics)

F3. Trust group potential and model neutrality

- Honor the wisdom of the group
- Encourage trust in the capacity and experience of others
- Vigilant to minimize the influence on group outcomes
- Maintain an objective, non-defensive, non-judgmental stance

As also mentioned earlier there is an alignment between the role of a Business Analyst too. The skills of a Business Analyst are published in the BABOK, and you can read about it on the website of the International Institute of Business Analysis (IIBA) http://www.iiba.org/babok-guide.aspx. They have seen the importance of facilitation skills, and have found it useful in their role, that has also tied up with the IAF.

Thus, it is clear that for a leader to be successful, biases are to be shunned, staying neutral and open to the groups wisdom, and the ability to "letting go" of their thoughts is essential. The need to be a competent facilitator is key. Organizations would benefit immensely if they built this into their leadership development practice. Educators would perhaps like to explore what they could do to ingrain facilitation skills amongst the students that they are working with, to prepare them to face the challenges of the VUCA world.

In the next chapter, we shall briefly list some scenarios where facilitation methods could work for a leader, and one can get familiar with some facilitation tools and techniques too. Some tips that can help one use these effectively are also shared. Although there are a vast range and number of such tools, we will focus on only some that are more useful and can get them started right away. Go ahead and make the most of it.

5
SCENARIOS WHERE THEY CAN BE DEPLOYED EFFECTIVELY

Facilitation, like any other skill, needs to be used at the right place, at the right time, with the right stakeholders, and in the right way, to be able to get the desired benefits. Over using it would slow down actions, and under using it would slow down results – both are not desirable.

It would thus make sense to know when it is appropriate to facilitate.

Some possible scenarios are detailed, and also some suitable tools and techniques that can be used are mentioned, though the detailed usage of these tools is detailed in the next chapter. Some of my past experiences also show that usage of these tools would need to be slightly modified or adapted before deploying them, to suit the variations in the situations.

Leaders need to help create a compelling vision and have the group aligned to it.

This could be at the organization level, Business Unit level, Cross Functional Team level, Project Team level, Own Team level. We have already seen how useful it would be to involve more stakeholders to create a vision. The vision creation may take more time, but save a lot more time in resolving conflicts around the execution later that would cause a lot more loss of time, and incidentally, it may also impact the quality of the products or services, and cause a lot of frustration and demotivation amongst the team members. My business partner Vinay often uses a phrase – " Go slow to go fast," and he facilitates many vision workshops. You can see that a small phrase like that, has such a deep thought through truth in it. What is needed here is for the leader to take some time to bring out all the diverse thoughts amongst the stakeholders, make all of it visible to them, and then have the group converge on to an agreeable and understandable vision? Agreeable with their hearts and minds, and not get swayed with the Abilene Paradox, and also important is that it is uniformly understandable so that there is one correct interpretation for all the stakeholders. Most often, these stakeholders need to cascade the vision down, and the leader would want to be assured that there is no disparity in understanding and that there is no miscommunication or misinterpretation along the way down. Some commonly used tools and techniques are Brainstorming, and Brainwriting, along with some innovative variations using pictures and drawings, would be useful. The first part of the Design Thinking approach and Systems Thinking methods would also be very useful.

The situations in which this needs to be done could also vary. We may have a new team getting formed, or a new leader taking charge, or one where multiple teams are being merged, or some addition of experts in a team, a change of direction for the team, are some examples of variations in this category. Sometimes there would be a need to have a vision getting adopted, and most often there would be a need to align this vision with the organization's vision and strategy.

Leaders need to help set goals

Goal setting was seen as a one on one interaction between the leader and the employee, and with the changes going on, the best results have been achieved where the team works together to break down their objectives and goals into tasks, understand the strengths of the team, and then set goals that would work in alignment with what the team as a whole is setting out to achieve. The KPI and KRA methods are now changing over to the OKR mode of working. Further, the annual goal-setting process is also not suitable anymore, as the goals are also changing very often, and hence these meetings need to happen many times over the year to stay relevant to the needs. A Focus Group Discussion methodology would be a good way to have these kinds of meetings produce effective results.

Some variants in this category are teams coming together for short durations on a project, and working with goals set for them, and hence over a year there could be goals that keep evolving; Agile meetings where goals are for as short as two weeks, and new goals keep getting established as the project is in progress, and of course, agile has become the norm and way of working in a lot of many organizations now.

Leaders need to establish Collaborative ways of working

Most work today involves expertise that is spread across functions in an organization. The dotted line reporting matrix system allows people to lend their experience where needed simultaneously. What makes it difficult is to manage the expectations and priorities between the cross-functional managers and the team members. Often, time is another important factor which pushes decision making to the limit. Lots of companies have spent a lot of money on building the culture of collaboration, and are investing in how to build leaders that can create a viable environment for it. Why would team members invest their time, if they are not going to gain anything out of it? Leaders often have to help groups establish the "why" of their work, and help the group see the impact of their prioritization, to realign towards organization's needs. Tools like the impact effort grid would be a great tool to use so that the group naturally come to a decision unanimously in helping them prioritize tasks and hence set a good environment to work in collaboration.

Variants that are probably very common are project-based collaboration, process update needs, and cultural alignment when two or more teams come together. There are also many situations where collaboration needs exist in parts of a project, rather than the whole project. In many cases, we also see pilot projects being done to showcase to the client and get their buy-in for the full project.

Leaders need to resolve conflicts

First leaders need to create the environment to harness ideas from the diversity that exists within the team, and this very need sets the grounds for conflicts. These conflicts if led to a good discussion and resolution, then it would result in great success. If not handled well enough, or handled from only the task side and ignoring the people side of it, else it could have disastrous outcomes. Conflicts around prioritization is perhaps a big one in this category of meetings. Conflicts around the distribution of workload, or around work-life balance are some other often seen too. Style differences, or process ambiguity, empowerment not clear, are all classic examples of this type of meeting needs. Some interesting facilitation tools around convergence methods are the criteria based grid and impact effort grid.

The conflicts could be between members of one team or different teams, and at times it could also be between two or more teams from different organizations.

In all situations where ideas, wisdom, analysis, and/or support, is needed, facilitation methods would be most appropriate. Whether it is a negotiation, driving innovation or any other situations where leaders need to get a group to do things together, they would need to harness the diverse knowledge in the group, establish processes that suit the diverse needs of the team, and empower them to be able to take decisions related to their deliverables. To be able to get full clarity about the real requirements associated with the goals, they would need to elicit information from people who would speak up and from people who would stay quiet. This calls for some good mix of facilitation tools related to divergence and convergence.

For leaders to think about where and when they could find it effective, let me share a little concept that Tom Wujec highlighted in his Ted Talk titled "Got a wicked problem – First tell me how you make toast." In this talk, he shares how wicked solving problems is all about working in groups to solve them. His research and some experiments showcased the concept of systems thinking that could help a leader get an improved outcome, rather than working with one knowledge expert or in members working in isolation. He showcased how first a leader could collate all the diverse ways, then get the group to interact to converge on one way forward. He showcases how group thinking in the right environment can create greater positive outcomes. A facilitator focuses on creating that right environment for a group to get to their desired outcomes. In other words, the use of facilitation skills by a competent facilitator would get groups aligned to solve problems in the best possible way.

He showcases how group thinking in the right environment can create greater positive outcomes. A facilitator focuses on creating that right environment for a group to get to their desired outcomes. In other words, the use of facilitation skills by a competent facilitator would get groups aligned to solve problems in the best possible way.

6
TIPS, TOOLS & TECHNIQUES

Facilitation is like any other skill; one needs to get started. It gets easier the more you use it. Initially, it may seem a bit awkward, but soon you will see yourself getting better at it, and that it brings some fantastic results. It is akin to the driving example, or the swimming one that we have probably heard many times earlier.

What is expected of a facilitator?

Facilitators, or should I say leaders in today's environment, lead by:

- Helping groups define their goals
- Helping groups determine their requirements
- Helping groups make a plan and help them accomplish those plans
- Helping groups arrive at great decisions that they buy in to
- Helping groups see multiple perspectives and then

find the optimum way forward
- Helping surface all assumptions so that there is a more precise understanding amongst the group
- Helping get groups to consensus in decision making
- Helping the group communicate fully and efficiently
- Helping create an environment of safety so that they can express all their thoughts and feelings
- Helping others take responsibility and then support them to live up to it
- Helping build other facilitators and leaders

Facilitators have a repository of tools and have some guiding behaviors that support facilitation. One can think of it like technical skills and behavioral skills. These guiding behaviors are the best practices that a facilitator should follow. They are:

Stay neutral on content, Manage the process

Trust the group, they have the knowledge or content, and seeing the way the current workforce has been groomed, they perhaps have deeper insights into content. As a leader, if you can focus on the process of getting the group to actively share information and avoid getting tempted to add information and create an environment of control on the content. At times, when the group is looking at you for content, you could use questioning skills to guide the group to the answers they seek. If you need to share, you could make suggestions rather than definitive directive statements. Even if this does not work, the facilitator could step in with some content, but after elaborately dramatizing it that they are temporarily stepping out of the facilitator role to help the group.

To provide clarity between content and process, Content is the what, and the process is the how. Content is all about the task, the subject, the problem, the agenda, the decision, the outcome; while Process is all about the methods, the maintaining of the relationships, the tools being used, the rules or norms being kept, the interaction dynamics about the group, the climate in the session.

Ask questions

A very good behavior to exhibit, and is the most important tool facilitative leaders should have. There are some very good questioning frameworks like the funnel technique, or ORID and Appreciative Inquiry. Good leaders use questioning to test assumptions, generate participation, gather information and probe for the unsaid or hidden points, getting to the cause of a problem, to name a few.

Listen actively

Leaders are as good as their listening ability. Listening actively means you exhibit genuine curiosity to understand. Of course, It also includes proper use of attentive body language, like leaning forward, eye contact. Prompting the quiet ones to speak is another important aspect, listening to the sounds of silence. When you show that you are listening actively, you could use acknowledgment, either as signals or with words, but also being aware of what is not being said, or who is not speaking; you could also paraphrase and provide more clarity through it, and additionally summarize at the end, are all great practices. Summarizing even when there are some long and complex statements is a good idea too, to ensure that nothing has been missed out or misunderstood by the group. Easy to say, a little hard to do, and with practice one would get better at it.

Be comfortable with silence

When asking especially reflective questions facilitators need to be very comfortable with silence. One needs to trust the group, and someone will break the silence and lead the way. This is even harder when the topic is loaded with high emotions and difficult situations of conflict. Having that extra patience can get the group to step up and break the deadlock.

Synthesize ideas

Great facilitators see that ideas start to get said, and it is also important to build on them so that it could be improved, if possible. Behaviors to support this sort of synthesizing will ensure that the outcome is the best possible one. Further, as people join, and support the building of ideas over conversations that they are part of, they start relating to the idea a lot more, and it then builds consensus, a post which it is easier to get people to commit to actions around it.

Test assumptions

Facilitators should always make all efforts to bring out any assumptions that people are working with and put it out in front of the group so that they can be clarified, corrected if needed, and clearly understood by everyone. It also ensures that everyone is aligned with what is being said and nothing left to diverse interpretations.

Make it visible

Making thoughts and ideas visible to the group increases participation. It is, therefore, a good idea to use boards, flipcharts, and sticky walls. It ensures that nothing is missed or sidelined, and everyone feels heard. It is like a little recording of ideas in progress and can serve as a documented version of the final decisions too. Capturing notes on a flip chart needs to be brief but clear, and as far as possible use the words of the person speaking about the idea. It would be best if, for the entire session, the notes are not only captured but kept visible to all the participants. It is often a challenge to record accurately and reflect exactly what the team said and meant and carefully avoid what the facilitative leader interprets the content and the meaning. Some of the facilitators who may have a challenge in spelling correctly as they capture, could use the spell check button and call out to the group that it is ok to use creative spelling as long as the group can understand things clearly and accurately.

Stay on track

It is often a challenge to maintain time when facilitating. A competent facilitative leader would take all needed efforts during the planning and executing of a session to ensure time is well utilized. We have all experienced meetings where at the end of the time set, we realize that we have not covered all that we needed to, or worse still, we have left out the most important parts. If timekeeping is a challenge, it would be good to ask a group member to act as the timekeeper for the session. Another challenge is when participants tend to digress from the topic, and there it is up to the facilitator to ensure that this is called out and steer the group back to the agenda. If the digression is relevant, it may be a good option to get it on to a separate parking lot and could be then dealt with later. It would be important to keep the parking lot in common sight of the group as well.

Give and receive feedback

This good practice is about "holding up a mirror" at regular intervals, to help the group see what is going on in the session and make corrections as suitable. Holding up the mirror is not just for the content but also for the feelings and emotions that are being brought out. Sometimes, holding up the mirror to bring out "silence" is also a great idea to get people to speak out and not hold back any thoughts. A good facilitator also seeks feedback periodically, especially about how things are going with the pace, the emotional state, the process, and the content. Basis the feedback, the facilitator should be able to adapt things to suit the group.

These behaviors, especially for a leader is a big paradigm shift, since the all the past eras of leadership, have had the leader on the forefront of speaking and sharing, rather than obtaining inputs from the group. These become even more difficult when the leader is also a subject matter expert and has significant experience. Breaking free of biases created by this and "acting dumb" in front of a group that they are leading, could be a very big challenge. Some simple ways to manage these challenges is by using a variety of facilitation process tools, and some of them are listed below, and also giving some simple guidelines on how to use them.

To be able to make use of the tools effectively it would be a good idea to discuss the elements of the environment and how to be able to suit the tools that could be deployed. As a simple example to illustrate the point, if the room is densely packed, and in a theatre-style seating with no space to move, it would not be possible to use methods where people have to form subgroups and exchange information between them, before sharing with the entire large group. One may then need to adapt or use some other methods that suit the setting available. All the elements that one needs to consider for facilitating effectively can be summed up in the SPACE Model.

SPACE is an acronym that stands for

    S – Social contracting
    P – Process
    A – Agenda and Outcomes
    C – Consider the environment (space and time)
    E – Engage the audience

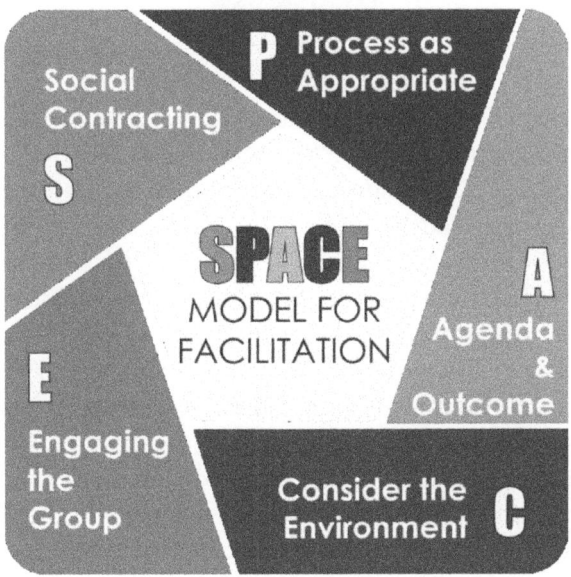

It is sometimes difficult to narrow down to the tools to use or when to use which tool and how do we think about it, and for this purpose, an illustration and an explanation to help narrow down your options are given below. This could serve as a guide.

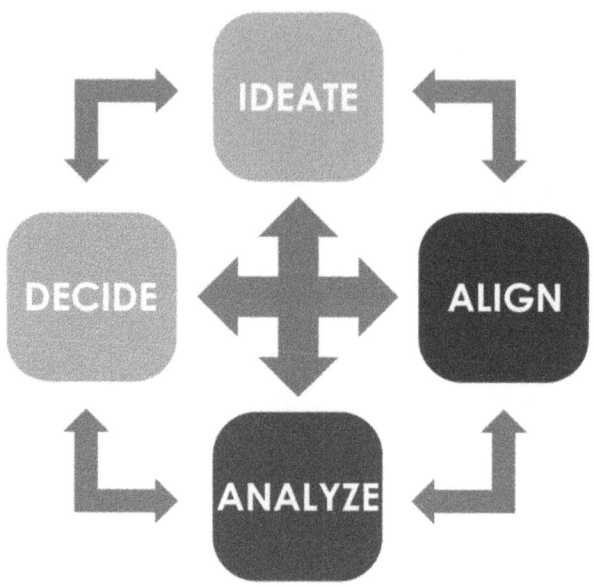

This simple framework for visualizing facilitation contains a lot of information. Firstly, the four boxes, labeled Ideate, Align, Analyze, and Decide, are the four broad categories of facilitation that a leader would face. Each category then has suggested tools that a leader could use to achieve that purpose. For example, if you need the group to ideate, you could use brainstorming, if you want them to align you could use focus group discussion, if you need them to analyze you could use force field, cause, or gap analysis, and if you want then to decide you can use multi-voting, criteria based or impact effort grid; and usually in a session you would use different combinations of these to suit the stage in the session you are on. The arrows if you notice, indicate that one could jump from one box to any of the other depending on the need, and there is no specific hierarchy or sequential order to follow. The other most important part is that you could start from any box, which is governed by the situation; however, you would have a clear box where you want to end, which is the purpose of the facilitated session situation.

For example, if you are trying to conclude on which particular product to buy, you know that you need to end at the decision box. Depending on if all the participants know about the products already then you may not need to run any process to align them, but if they are not clear about it, then you would have to use a process and establish the alignment. Similarly knowing the purpose of the selection of the product, or the extent of some improvement needed, or details about the problem that one is trying to solve, based on the situation on hand, the starting point could be decided, the final step is pre-decided based on the objective of the facilitated session.

Facilitation Process Tools

Visioning

This is a highly interactive and engaging approach for a group to come together to clarify their thoughts and share ideas with each other, and to jointly create a shared vision statement of the desired future or the to-be state. This tool allows people to put across their ideas and makes sure everyone is engaged and has had the opportunity to provide their inputs. This process can be deployed in very creative ways to create energy, and it gets people aligned as they creatively come up with the desired vision statement.

The Process

Step 1: Place a set of questions that relate to the subject and asking about how the desired end state should look like. These questions would be different depending on the situation, and the example below can be used and adapted as needed.

Example: Sample visioning questions about improving the user experience of online shopping.
- What specific improvements have we made
- What specific outcome have we achieved
- What problems have we solved
- What are the users saying about us
- What are the feelings and emotions of the users
- How are all the people behaving

Step 2: Having chosen the question or questions, ask the participants to imagine the future state. This is also referred to as "future back" process. In the above example, say "imaging that we have achieved the user experience of online shopping and we are now meeting to discuss the situation." Having got the participants in that state of thinking, place the questions you have selected or created.

Step 3: Get each person to individually respond to these questions, without talking to the others in the session. Ensure that you give them enough time, say 10 minutes, to reflect and capture clear details.

Step 4: Ask participants to form small groups and share with each other and consolidate to represent the group's response on one flipchart or sheet, per group. Allow for about 5 minutes for the group to share and consolidate.

Step 5: If you have many groups (6 or more), then you could merge two group to form new slightly larger groups repeat step 3. You may now need only 3 minutes for them to consolidate. (if the number of groups is fewer than 5, this step could be skipped.)

Tip: You could also ask each people to put up their answers on the sticky wall, ask the group to reflect on the themes they see, and then move ahead for the group to take the lead and word a vision statement.

Step 6: Get each group to share with the larger audience in the room. Allow for participants to seek clarity as the responses are being shared. You will find that the group has an aligned vision.

Step 7: Get the group to consolidate all the inputs into a sentence (or maybe two sentences). Allow some time for them to wordsmith and come up with a final answer that everyone is comfortable with.

Step 8: This is the vision statement that the group has come up with, and which they all see as the goal they need to attain.

It would also be useful to know about variants to this method, especially useful when you need to have the anonymity of the person giving the idea. This is especially useful when the group consists of people who may not be comfortable talking in the presence of others in the group, and the requirement is to create an environment of safety.

Brainstorming

This is a simple process that perhaps many of us have led or participated in earlier and we would be reasonably familiar too. It is a way to get better ideas and different unique ones to then compare and choose from. It is also a very creative exercise that allows for everyone to participate and place their ideas before a group without the fear of it being challenged. As it separates evaluation from creativity, this is often used to challenge traditional ways of working or thinking, and coming up with some "out of the box" ideas, and has the potential to come up with a wide range of solutions to problems being faced.

The Process

Step 1: Announce that the group is going to engage in brainstorming and set up the rules.
Example of some commonly used rules:

- Suspend judgment or evaluation until later
- Let ideas flow freely
- No idea is a bad idea
- Build on the ideas of others
- Think differently and creatively
- Be humorous
- Everyone participates
- Don't hold back any idea, however crazy it may sound

You could also seek the group's inputs to set the rules, which generally works better.

Step 2: provide the topic or the problem statement and allow for a couple of minutes for people to think in silence.

Step 3: Brainstorming can now begin. You could go in a specific order, or even popcorn style, and keep listing all the ideas until everyone has shared all their thoughts. Sometimes it is useful to pause for a minute and ask for more ideas, as there could be some more thoughts triggered based on what was said.

Step 4: Ideas are captured as called out, and it is good to make it visible to everyone.

Step 5: Discuss each idea captured in detail, so that everyone understands it clearly. It is a good idea to group ideas that are the same and just worded differently.

Step 6: If you have a longer than the desired list, use voting to shortlist the ideas that the group wants to try out, to a size that would be desired. In case, there is a need to prioritize, additional steps around decision making using criteria grid or impact effort grid could be used.

Step 7: Finalize the list which should by now be in consensus with the group.

You will find that you have created the environment where everyone feels valued, and they also have come up with a list of possible options to take further and are also supportive of trying out these new ways of working.

Focus Group Discussion

This is a structured conversation with a carefully selected group of participants that produce qualitative comments to be able to provide clarity and to have the group have an aligned understanding of all the perspectives around it. This is usually followed up with an analysis or decision making technique as well. It is advisable to conduct these in group sizes of 6 – 10 participants. Larger groups tend to stretch for too long and often dilutes the focus. This technique can be used in situations where you are helping the group describe job processes, job hand-off points, and overall workflows, get a clearer understanding on what is the need to solve a particular problem, etc..

The Process

Step 1: Pose an open-ended question to the group.

Some examples are

- What would make your job easier (desired to-be state)
- How do you currently do your job (current as-is state)

Step 2: Ask for verbal ideas and encourage the group to build on them, and to provide the level of detail required. Capture these ideas on a chart. If it can be pictorially depicted, that would be helpful too, especially if it is a process flow.

Step 3: Based on the need, this may then have to move to analysis or decision making, for which other techniques would need to be used.

Variants around using this process effectively with a homogeneous group or a heterogeneous group would be good to keep in mind too. One would need to be very clear about the people invited to this session, as you need everyone connected with the topic, and no one else, and also to keep it within a manageable size.

Joint Application Design

This is very similar to the focus group discussion technique, except that it has a different purpose and therefore a different set of participants. The purpose of a JAD, as it is popularly called, is to find flaws in a design or a prototype. The participant profile is usually a group of experts from various groups that would be stakeholders to the design or prototype, and the group is asked to find all flaws from their perspectives. When this is shared, the design can be relooked at, to think of changes to it that when done would work for everyone. The process steps are similar to the focus group discussion one.

Needs and Offers: This is a method to get a constructive dialog in a group to help people move to action. Where you see engagement levels lower than expected or speed is slower than desired, or members in the team are feeling disengaged and not pulling their weight, are some good situations where this technique can get you the desired results.

The Process

Step 1: Establish the focus of the exercise, call out the observations and the reason for the session, by sharing (or asking the sponsor to share) the goal of the organization, where the group is currently at, and what are the indicators that suggest that a change is needed.

Step 2: Explain the process in detail, about the focus around needs first, and then offers.

Step 3: Start with the first part of the process, ask individuals to list out all their individual needs which when provided for would have them contribute more to the organization's goals. Ensure that they write one need per sticky note, and as many sticky notes as they need. It is usually a good idea to use one color sticky notes for the needs. Give them 10 minutes. Ask them to put up all their needs on the wall in front of the room.

Step 4: Ask the participants to have a good look at all the needs that have come up. Allow enough time for the group to talk about the needs listed and get clarity of what the needs mean, and get them to cluster similar ideas together by moving the sticky notes as appropriate.

Step 5: Ask the participants to now think about what they are willing to offer the organization that may be useful to deal with some of the needs that they have seen. Provide a different color sticky notes this time, and ask them to write their offers, one per sticky note, and as many sticky notes as they would like along with their name (explain that the name would help the team reach out to take their offers to support the needs). Give them 5 minutes. Ask them to put up all their offers on the wall in front of the room.

Step 6: Ask the group to have a look at the offers made, allow them to seek clarifications if they need.

Step 7: Ask the participants to connect with people they see who can offer something to support and provide for their need, and have a conversation and set up the next steps for their needs. This is a matchmaking step. Depending on the volume of needs and offers, sufficient time needs to be factored for it.

At this stage, you should have created a few connects to have some needs met or planned to resolve. You can help the group find ways to support and help each other.

In some cases, it would be a good idea to check back with them if they are on track with their needs and whether the other group is living up to its offers made.

It is also possible to run this across larger audience with diverse needs, and when the needs of individuals are made visible, once can seek volunteers to provide offers to meet their needs. This simple matchmaking exercise can get some actions within the group that would have positive outcomes.

Force Field Analysis

This analytical tool is a structured way to analyze forces that act favorably to the needs and other forces that act counter to the needs. When there is a very large problem at hand, then this approach would be suitable. One could break down the forces acting, and then for the smaller forces, individual strategies to deal with them can emerge. It can allow participants to filter what areas they can focus on to overcome their problem, rather than looking it at in a large block and finding it too big to deal with.

The Process

Step 1: Call out the problem statement and title your flip chart with it. Help the group identify the desired state and the current state. Write these at the top and the bottom of the flip chart respectively and draw a horizontal line at the middle.

Step 2: Identify forces that favor the move to the desired state and write those at the lower half of the flip chart with arrows next to them pointing upwards indicating the direction that the forces are acting. Now identify forces that obstruct the move to the desired state and write those at the upper half of the flip chart with arrows next to them pointing downwards indicating the direction that the forces are acting. This makes the visual complete of what are the smaller forces to deal with.

Step 3: Now the group can be led into a discussion on which of these forces are a priority and could be dealt with, one could use an impact effort grid to arrive at the prioritization.

Step 4: Seek volunteers for each of the priority areas identified.

You should now have some actionable steps and people to work on them for an otherwise complex problem that seems too big to deal with.

Root Cause Analysis

A simple and often used analysis tool to identify the causes of a situation rather than seeing and working with the easily visible symptoms. When a problem persists, or when a situation is sensed to be very critical, a little time invested in cause analysis could save a lot of heartburn in the future, as it can lead to a final definitive solution. Using a fishbone diagram to depict cause and effect, or by probing with the 5-Why technique are good ways to surface the causes.

It is important here, to help the group differentiate between causes and effects. Usually, once the group has identified all causes, the group can get to brainstorming solutions for all of them.

Gap Analysis: This is a technique used to help groups identify blocks that prevent them from achieving the goal. It helps to identify or surface any missing steps from the current position to move to the desired goal.

The Process

Step 1: Identify the desired state. Either a Visioning exercise or a Focus Group Discussion could be sued for it. Make sure that the desired state is fully detailed, to provide the visibility and later assist in identifying what may be missing. Has this posted on a flip chart / sticky wall at the right-hand corner?

Step 2: Identify the current state. Have this captured and placed in the left-hand corner. Ensure that all details are captured.

Step 3: Participants are now asked to focus on finding gaps. Ask members to work in small groups and surface gaps that they notice.

Step 4: Get all groups to share, eliminate duplicates as they share, and have the final list captured in full detail and have that put in between the two charts.

This is usually followed with brainstorming or Focus Group Discussion on how to deal with the gaps that have surfaced.

You should now have helped the group identify gaps and find ways to deal with them.

Multivoting

A very commonly used decision-making tool, that helps get a decision in consensus. Often used to sort a long list of suggestions or ideas and to prioritize them, and also sometimes to make the one final choice from a list of options.

The Process

Step 1: Clarify the list of items that are to be prioritized or selected. This could be a list from an earlier brainstorming session, or a force field analysis too. Have members discuss the advantages and disadvantages of each of them, so that the group has the same level of information for them to think through when making their selection.

Step 2: Identify the criteria and purpose of their voting. This is to ensure that they vote with an aligned purpose.

Example:

- The easiest items to take up
- The highest business impact items to select
- The fastest turnaround items to accept
- The most valuable items for the customer

Step 3: Each person is given a specific number of points (usually 100) and asked to distribute their points across the list. It is useful to place some restrictions like no more than 50% to one item, and no less than 20%, as it could eliminate biases and also think through the purpose alignment of the ideas before distributing it fairly from their perspective. Participants are then asked to gather around the list, think it through and allocate their points.

Step 4: Total the points allocated to each item on the list

to identify priorities or selection.

This is a democratic process, and it allows for the elimination of pressure and bias, as it ensures that there are no winners and losers. It leaves the participants feeling that they can live with the outcome.

Criteria Grid

This technique is very useful in helping a group arrive at a final decision in selecting one option, and in consensus. It is a common thing to see that no one solution can meet all the needs of a group, while one would be useful to some, others would want something else. In such a situation when you have a difference of opinion in a group, getting them to a consensus and with the impact that there are no winners or losers, but have agreed on what is the best option, is a great outcome, and this technique gets you exactly that.

The Process

Step 1: Share all the options from which the group needs to pick one. If needed, for alignment, a discussion on the advantages and disadvantages of each of them could be had.

Step 2: List all the option like a list on the extreme left of the flip chart, under the heading "options."

Step 3: Get the group to share all the critical criteria that are to be kept in consideration for the selection. List them vertically alongside the heading of options already created. It would be a good idea to restrict the number of criteria to a maximum of about 5. Draw horizontal and vertical lines to make it a multi-column grid of rows and columns. Add one more column at the extreme right-hand side and mark the heading for this as "total."

Step 4: Looking at all the criteria, ask the group to assign a weight for each criterion. Usually get them to distribute 100 points across all the criteria, and mark the agreed weights against each criterion in the box.

Step 5: Get the group to rank the options basis the first criteria only, from 1 to n (n being the number of options in the list) with the lowest ranked (worst case rank) as 1, and going upwards thereon. Mark the ranks in the respective box on the grid. Repeat for the next criteria and go on until all criteria are ranked.

Step 6: Now multiply the rank with the weightage and write that value in the grid box.

Step 7: Total the values of the first option in the grid box horizontally and have the final total in the column marked as a total. Repeat for the next option, and go on until you complete the list of options.

Step 8: The highest total in this column is the selected option for the group.

This process ensures that everyone has shared their perspectives and evaluated based on weighted criteria, and the selection eventually arrived at is the one that works best for the group.

Impact Effort Grid

This is a technique that is used to help the group prioritize their list of tasks to be accomplished. Often there is a disagreement on what options are to be prioritized, especially when there is a list where everything looks useful and good. To help a group to come to a consensus methodically to prioritize is when this tool is commonly deployed.

The Process

Step 1: Draw a 2 x 2 grid / matrix.

Step 2: Label the horizontal axis as a business impact, and mark the line from low to high, with high being on the right. Label the vertical axis as the effort needed, and mark this line from a low to high, with high being up.

Step 3: Ask the group to take all the tasks and ask them to discuss and rate each one of them on the grid considering both impact and effort. Get them to post their conclusions on the grid.

Step 4: What you get as tasks in the low effort and high business impact, are the tasks that need to get done first.

What you have got the group to look at is what are the tasks that need little effort but would yield great business impact. These are quick and large wins. You also have other tasks where effort needed is low, and the business impact is also low; and a similar box where both are high. These can be discussed based on the situational need to determine which box needs to get prioritized. The last box with high effort and the low business impact would be the lowest priority and can be discarded or taken up at the very last.

This approach, is very participative and everyone is involved in the decision making, and hence when they get back to executing these tasks, there is alignment and no biases of any kind. The why of the prioritization is made clear in a very democratic manner.

Please note: If you would like a more detailed and illustrative step by step guide, along with variants, when and how to run them, please register and download from **www.facileader.com** for free.

7
THREE STORIES

Strategy from the bottom up

The year was 2001, markets in the US were getting competitive, and organizations were cutting operating costs by outsourcing work to lower-cost regions like India and the Philippines. The pressure on many of the large companies in the US was further mounting, and after they had outsourced a lot of things, they were still being pushed to find creative ways to manage costs even in their core key areas of operations. These companies were reluctant to outsource these, as they feared the loss of control and quality compromises. They were speaking to many global consulting firms to see how they could set up shop in these lower cost regions of the world themselves.

Ravi, had just joined a company, Insource (names changed for privacy reasons) whose business was captive offshoring, in other words, they would bring companies based out of US into India, and set up a back office for them, and then insource some key processes that were erstwhile outsourced to third-party back-office service providers. The business model offered ground support and not just advise. The scope of work was to lead the setting up of these centers from a green field state, that is, Insource was responsible for the setting up of the infrastructure to the standards governed by the customer, hire the people as required, transit the processes for execution from the center, build the profitability, and the leadership succession; and with all these done, they would transit to the new leader and exit. All of this at a fee. It seemed like a great model and timed right from all the market trend surveys and other research indications, and Ravi was all excited. Ravi had had a lot of experience running back offices, and he had even successfully turnaround a few of these BPOs by optimizing their operations and ways of working. Insource had a healthy pipeline of prospective customers who were actively exploring this model, many of which were names from the Fortune 500 companies.

The sales team at Insource had very experienced and well-connected people located both in India and the US. Ravi was tracking the pipeline, and he was surprised that many of them dropped out at the last few stages of the sales cycle. The sales team thought it apt to include him in the selling of the "India story" as they felt that this could perhaps influence the decision favorably. He supported the team by putting together information about India, as directed, that was included in the sales pitch, and he even presented this with all the passion behind it, and had answers to all the questions that came up in the meetings. However, the dropout from the pipeline continued.

With a good part of one year has gone by, and with no success, Ravi was wondering what the future holds for Insource and himself. The entire sales team was feeling very demotivated, and to help build the spirits up, the entire team at Insource decided to have an off-site meeting to discuss the situation. Ravi stepped up to moderate the discussions.

Before the meeting date, Ravi did a quick check in with the Directors and got their views on what they were expecting out of the meeting. He got their approval for seeking inputs for any strategy level suggestions for sales to win deals. With a clear objective in mind, Ravi had a plan in place.

The meeting convened, and Ravi first ran a quick emotion check, and he found that everyone was feeling very low and he approached this with a visioning exercise. He got all of them to close their eyes, and imagine what the scenario would look like in two years, if they have a sign up from a client, and they have gone into the execution mode. He then asked them to share on sticky notes the different emotions that surface for them, guiding them to write each emotion on separate sticky notes. He had all these notes put together on the wall, and got the group to spend a few minutes looking at it. He then asked a question – "do we want to make this happen?" Of course, he got a yes response to it. He then played this up and said – "I can't hear the response," and he immediately got a loud yes from everyone. He then used a long pause and made eye contact with everyone in the room, and went on to say – "ok, then let's get to work and figure out a strategy that would help us get there." He now had everyone focused and energetic. He recognized that setting the context and the environment is critical for facilitation to be successful, and he had just done that brilliantly.

He then started with the force field analysis technique. He got the desired state declared by the group. They came up with "Three client signups in three years." He also got the current state declared by the group, which of course, was "Struggling to get the first sign up." Having set this up on a large flipchart and put it up on the wall for everyone to see, he drew a line across the middle of the flipchart, and arrows underneath pointing up to indicate significant forces and arrows on top pointing down to indicate the hindering forces.

He shared the meaning of the arrows and asked people to name these forces that help and hinder.

After a few responses, he probed some of them with questions until they came up with a force description that was something that could be dealt with. One example of this was when a participant mentioned customer comfort, he probed further for what that meant, and he eventually got the response from the group, that the customer felt that Insource had nothing to lose in the entire deal, whereas the customer would be taking a risk in dealing with a company that has not done this before, and had relatively lower credibility compared to the big consulting companies.

This force was put forth to the group and asked them for ideas on dealing with it. While brainstorming, many unique and creative ideas got tabled. Ravi ensured that no one would react to the ideas, and instead just make a long list. Later, he got the group to look at multi-voting as a method to prioritize the ideas. The one that came up as the most popular was "put our skin in the game" which when expanded meant that we could offer to co-invest in the India entity with the client, and have a pre-defined exit policy that incorporates all the wants of the customer – number of employees, number of successfully transited processes, building the leadership succession, and on exit receive a pre-defined value of the investment. This idea was then presented to the Directors, and they accepted it and went ahead with changing the sales pitch accordingly. The response was tremendous, and their first win on this new sales pitch came up in less than two months, and they have had multiple wins come in soon after as well. Today, the company has a great business model with very impressive clients.

Questions to reflect upon – What made the difference? What does it take to exhibit this kind of leadership?

Alignment Concerns

Harish (name changed for privacy reasons) had this idea for an app, that would serve as a question/quiz, where questions could be generated, and users would respond to it with their answers. This could serve as a test, assessment, or just knowledge enhancement. This could then be integrated into different sectors like education, healthcare, tourism, entertainment, and many other possibilities too. He put together a team of 3 other contacts of his, all coming from different backgrounds – HR, IT, Marketing, and he himself had vast experience in operations. A great idea, an excellent diverse team, a winning formula for a startup.

They were geographically spread out and working from four different cities of the globe. They managed to connect regularly virtually, and built the pilot, and had it launched in a small control group of about 1000 users. The reviews were terrific, and they were feeling good that their hard work and the investments made was working for them. They were now ready to take it to the next level and were keen to look for some venture funding, sensing the vast potential that the product had.

On approaching the VCs, Harish realized that if they had to get one to invest, they would need a success story or two, without which the VCs were not keen, and those that were slightly interested offered valuations that were very low.

The four of them decided to put in a little more of their own funding, and all of them stretched, dipping into their reserves that had been set aside for a rainy day, and pooled it all in. All of them were emotionally very high as they had good reviews, and at the same time were concerned about the stretch they had made with the investments. Each of them was keen to close some success case so that they could then get the VCs in, and get back their reserves quickly.

Keeping all of this in mind, in the next call, the de-facto leader Harish, provided some data around the education sector as he felt that it had high potential and natural market to enter into, besides he was very passionate about it too. He asked the team to start working towards it and connect with people they knew in this sector. They were to review progress on it weekly and had set aside a time of 4 weeks to be able to get the first case signed up. In their next weekly call, there was no progress by anyone. Having reinforced the need to get further quickly on this, he pushed again. He was hoping that the next week would be better.

In the next call, everyone was surprised that no progress had been made, and everyone had justifiable reasons why they could not get any connects. One of the team members spoke up, and he said that it would be good if he can get on to the tourism sector, as he had a few contacts there and one of them was also part of the pilot user group. Another wanted to connect with the entertainment sector as she had a similar story to offer. Finally, Harish had to very reluctantly concede and get them to go in areas that they were comfortable in. He was worried how this might impact the operations as the orders close, but then hoping that it would all work out and to stay positive with all the others on the team he gave his consent.

In the next weekly call, they had made progress and had interests coming up in both tourism and entertainment areas. The team was all excited again. They could imagine the future as the VCs would invest large sums based on the success in not one but two sectors. Harish was excited as he could see his dream of buying a house starting to seem real. The others all had their dreams too, a luxury villa in Dubai, around-the-world holiday with family, funding for higher education for their child; all starting to become real. The conversation tone was very positive and enthusiastic. Everyone was excited about what good news they would hear next week.

The next weekly came up, and everyone was excited, they had all logged in five minutes earlier itself. The good news came from all three sectors now – as Harish had also managed to get one buy-in from a university that wanted to explore options, the tourism ministry of a state provided an opportunity to do a trial, and the local theatre group wanted to see how they can make use of this app. What a week that was.

Little did they realize that the spread that happened meant they had to put in more money to be able to service all of them. This dawned on them soon. In a mid-week connect they made to discuss this, it was unanimously decided that each of them would raise the fund on their individual capacity and support the next phase. They managed to get some personal loans and invest. They were confident that the day was now not far when they would see success.

Now came the real challenge, and this was something Harish had anticipated but did not share, as he did not want to dampen the spirits. He was from the operations background and new that operations would spread out too thin and would be a struggle. He was hoping that he would manage somehow.

Soon, pressure on delivering to all three needs came up, and the group started having their conflicts. Each one was pushing for their project to be closed, and technically it was a big challenge as the three sectors all needed a few significant changes to align with the sector needs. The conflicts grew, and over the next three weeks, they started losing trust as they perceived personal agenda are coming in the way of their business decisions on the projects.

Eventually, the team split. A team that had a great product

idea, great potential, proven success, could not make it to the next step.

Questions to reflect upon – What could have been done to manage this situation? What kind of a mindset would a leader need to handle these situations?

Leadership Succession Challenge

A large NGO group that was doing fantastic work in many areas of community service was going through a crisis to get their members taking on leadership roles.

A group of over 130 members, all of them who have been leaders in their profession, in a very smoothly functioning NGO, had the practice of year on year changing their leaders. This NGO had a focus on five verticals of service, and each vertical had multiple projects. Each project or a collection of similar projects was managed by a committee led by a chairperson of the committee. Their progress was monitored by a Director responsible for each vertical, who was eventually reported to the board, headed by the nominated President who would also serve for one year in that role. The members were also volunteers, and contributed, time, money, and provided leadership and guidance to the projects.

This entity was consistently growing year on year and was known to be a model NGO that many aspired to replicate, or better if they could join and be part of it itself.

As their projects got more prominent, and more projects get added, the work also grew much more significant. More time and money was needed, besides a strong drive from the committee members of each project. Being a voluntary organization, the challenge was no member could be forced into action, and the need was to inspire them, influence them, and engage them. In the past, the Directors of each of the verticals chose people as Chairperson, and their committee members, based on what they knew about each of the members. Members were then tasked to get some activities done in the projects they were nominated into. Many members who mainly did not emotionally connect with the projects, were quite reluctantly delivering, and hence the quality of the work was declining as well. The work seemed like a hard task and a chore that many did not want to engage in. The group was seeing some projects doing exceptionally well, especially when they had the committee members all self-driven and committed to the projects they were associated with. In short, it was unpredictable about how the projects would turn out each year. Those who were seen to do excellent work, rose up to take on higher level roles. Being self-motivated on projects of all kinds is definitely not easy for everyone, and when you are dealing with members who are all successful business leaders, they divert their time into other areas of interest to them. This over time resulted in a reduced engagement, and in their informal survey, they found that they had only about 30% of the members active and engaged, which was half of what the number was about two years earlier. This resulted in another associated problem, when fewer people are engaged, raising the needed funds to execute projects was becoming challenging, and the required number of leaders to run the number of projects they had was becoming a challenge. This was further getting complicated when each President in his or her tenure was expanding the scope as much as possible in their year.

They then decided that they had to find a way to engage members a lot more and showcase that leadership is not as time-consuming as was now being perceived.

They decided to change their approach of how people take on work in the system. They got all the members together for a workshop that was facilitated by one member. They first looked at a timeline to see how their projects and project needs have grown and compared it with how their membership had grown. The group got a sense of what was involved and how the ratio of members to the projects was quite standard, however, when they compared it with the engagement scores and saw the dip, they realized what the root cause was.

The next question in the session naturally then went on to – how do we engage our members more actively. A lot of system-related and process related ideas came about, and many were found practical, and they were shortlisted for action. The discussion then went on the member's roles itself, and the group went through a process of needs and offers, where members stated what they needed to be more engaged and what they would like to offer to get engaged and engage others. As this list got fully laid out, they arrived at some clarity on where to involve whom, and the new incoming board could then align their plans accordingly.

A shift in the engagement score was evident, as more people started participating in areas of their liking, and as it aligned with the projects of their choice, their commitments to it rose significantly. As they got more engaged, people now started volunteering to lead committees as well, and hopefully, soon we would have resolved the challenges of both engagement and leadership succession. This trend was encouraging, and as they go through a few more iterations, they should be back in full speed, and not only that the NGO would run better, but many areas of the community would significantly improve as well.

Questions to reflect upon – Do we have similar situations in our regular work that we do? How can we lead our teams to higher engagement?

PART THREE: COMPETENT FACILITATORS ARE NATURAL LEADERS

In the world that is fast changing, where the leader is faced with VUCA challenges, it is clear that the most valuable skill of a leader is Facilitation.

This involves a mindset that is open to new ways of thinking and doing. It involves being neutral truly and totally and open to diversity. With this mindset, if they can pick up the technical side of facilitation, looking at divergence and convergence methods, appreciative inquiry methods, and focused on group outcomes, one can easily pick up tools and techniques and master them. Being open to feedback and continuous learning would help them accelerate towards mastery.

Facilitators need to be self-aware, to sense when they are not as comfortable as they should be, so that they can take that extra effort to continue to be facilitative. They need to be socially aware, to sense the emotions in the group individually and collectively so that they can think of what they need to change to get the group to the desired emotional state. They need to exhibit focused agility; they cannot be stuck to the planned process, they need to adapt to the group's needs, even temper the speed if needed, give space when needed, and push ahead when needed. They need to have the commitment that they want to achieve the desired outcome, and commit to it, even at the risk of them being misjudged.

People who demonstrate this level of courage and confidence are undoubtedly competent facilitators, and are very clearly natural leaders, as they can lead all kinds of groups, overcoming, various kinds of constraints and hurdles, towards desirables outcomes. Precisely what a leader is expected to do, and hence competent facilitators are natural leaders.

In this part, we delve a little deeper to explore how easily and quickly we can build proficiency in facilitation, and also share some ways to get more information to support in this journey.

8
IS IT REALLY A NEW SKILL?

Is Facilitation such a new or a different unique skill? This may be a question on your mind.

Remember a time when your teacher asked the class to come up with a decision on where they would like to go for a two-day tour. Someone in the class would have taken the lead, and got the group to come to a consensus.

Recall a time when as a family you had to plan for a vacation, someone would have led the discussion and got the family to agree on a few things, and then the plan would have got done.

You may have experienced a situation when you were reached out to, to resolve a conflict between two of your friends, and you would have got them to share and see each other's viewpoints and perspectives, and eventually solved the problem.

A child wanting something that was not possible, and how the parent would convince the child to drop the idea, is another scenario that is very common.

As part of a team, you may have come across diverse opinions, and then had someone step up to get the group to align in one direction.

The list is endless, and all these were in some way facilitated. Even some of the facilitation techniques probably have been used, whether or not you may have named the techniques.

Subconsciously, we are all facilitators and have facilitated many situations in our lives. All we need to do is to make it a practice, as we lead our teams. It is just a matter of knowing, and then practicing it regularly, knowing that it can bring about the best outcomes. This of course, in the current changing environment becomes even more critical.

Tom Wujec, in his YouTube video – "Got a Wicked Problem? First, tell me how you make toast" showcases the power of facilitation. He shows how easy it is to put together a problem to a group, and seeing how they can collectively come to a great outcome. He had put together a research collection of drawings made by a target set of individuals in describing through a drawing on how they make toast. The different and diverse depictions are analyzed for the common traits, and he brings out how humans naturally think. How we think, and how we think as a group, and how a group eventually comes to a consensus. Getting a group to a consensus is the sole purpose of facilitation.

When a skill relates to how we normally think and function, it is definitely, an easy skill to develop and master.

We see so many nations following democracy system of politics. Why would this be so popular and likable? People relate to it as the most convenient way to work and interact amongst a group. Facilitation is about getting the best out of a democracy system, and this is more and more the culture in organizations.

Sales, something that has existed since times immemorial. This is all about giving a choice and people selecting what works best for them. Facilitation is about making all the options visible, so people can choose what works best.

Again, I could keep going on and on, but the point is clear – facilitation has been around, we have all done it, we have all participated in it, and now for a leader, it is all about practicing it where it is needed the most – in their environment of leadership.

In my last job, one key part of my role was to build leaders who would take over my work from me, in other words, I had to work myself out of my job. I had successfully managed to do this eight times in 3 years, as I handed over startups that I had to build based on pre-decided contract agreements with my clients. What I realized is that I enjoyed the task of up-skilling leaders more than I cared about the business, and that was when I stepped out to start a business that would focus on helping leaders excel. Picking from the experience of helping build leaders, it very soon dawned on me that each person is unique and has different ways of leading, and yet the common thread I saw was that they were all successful when they took into consideration inputs from their teams and got the team to support in the final decision that they took together which saved them from the struggle otherwise they would have to go through in implementing the decision. Further, with the VUCA challenges pushing for dynamic changes, the pain of change management was reduced considerably. Creating the facilitation culture also rubbed off down the hierarchy, and the creation of a facilitation culture in the organization paid rich dividends in terms of adapting to the environment. It certainly marked a clear shift in the leadership era, and yet the shift seemed very natural and simple. It was simply a matter of adapting to the mindset of a facilitator – one that can get the groups wisdom into leadership decision making.

In this exciting journey, I trained, mentored, coached, and facilitated, and realized the power of facilitation. I was lucky to have got introduced to the professional facilitation world and went to get myself certified as a Certified Professional Facilitator (CPF) which is a credential issued by International Association of Facilitators (IAF). The qualification by itself may not mean much, but the association with this professional body, and networking with the colleagues who practice facilitation, has taught me so many new things about facilitation, so many new processes, so many new situations, and so many new methods to apply to various needs, that it continually helps me get even better at facilitation. For those who would like to check it out – www.iaf-world.org is their website.

When we also look at how this links to the Maslow's Hierarchy of Needs, leaders today need to adapt to the needs that have evolved to the next level, and the same level of evolution is also felt by each of us, and thus it is all about treating the team members like we would want them to treat us. Comparing this evolution with the evolution of leadership is depicted in the illustration below. Although it seems like a paradigm shift, facilitation is, in reality, a natural way any person would lead in the VUCA times.

THE FACILITATIVE LEADER

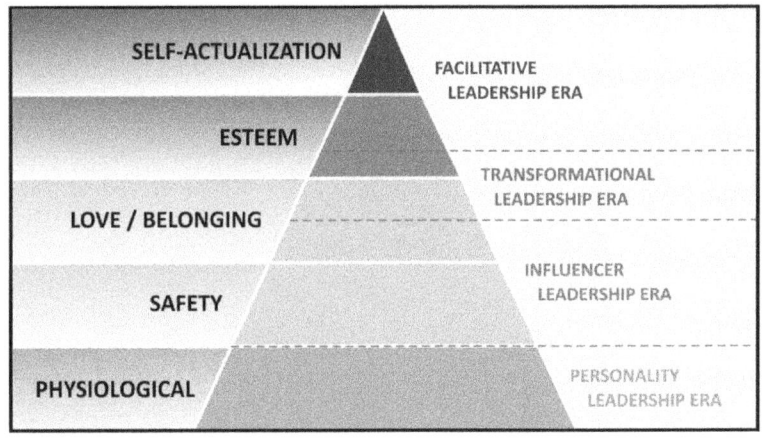

MASLOW'S HIERARCHY OF NEEDS   **LEADERSHIP EVOLUTION**

In the next chapter, we shall discuss how this skill can be learned and how we can get better as we regularly use it in our day to day activities.

SANJAY DUGAR

9
IT CAN BE LEARNT EASILY

As I have been interacting with people from all walks of life, in my quest in helping leaders excel, I have seen most of them start out and get good at facilitation in a very short time. When I had circled back to have conversations with them, when I happened to meet them socially, I noticed that their regular conversations itself being very facilitative, almost like facilitation becoming their second nature. One case, that to me was a complete shift, and a major transformation of the individual, I shall narrate here.

A large packed ready to eat foods manufacturing company was started by a first-time entrepreneur, Arvind (name changed for privacy reasons), who gradually built the business, in a very competitive environment, competing with some of the very large globally known players. Coming from a background of distributing FMCG products in the country, and realizing the demand for top quality products, got into the manufacturing sector. In a short span of 12 years, he established the company as a strong brand. The company was entirely built on the vision of Arvind, who with his humble style of leadership got the best of people to work for him, and got a very loyal customer base. His core strength was his quality-based philosophy, and he chose not to fight competition on price, which was the norm for most entrants competing against established players. He chose to go the value-selling route. Realizing the value that he could add to his customer base, through a strong research team, he added the R&D department to further his vision and bring in new products that would cater to the increasing needs of the consumers. Soon, the company established an unshakeable numero uno position in the country. Having got this far, the attempt to further enhance the lead over the next few ranked players crept in.

In his attempt to grow the market share, he quickly added more manufacturing plants, got a larger distribution network in place, all of this was easy as his brand was a sought-after brand, and many wanted to be part of this successful journey. He had stretched to the limit in loans to be able to fast-track the growth. The markets were also showing positive trends, the market for packed ready to eat foods were predicted to grow substantially over the visible future years. It was all set for a major leap to the next level. However, he started encountering problems.

The sales teams were bringing in the business, but the inventory was of a very different product mix, and this was forcing the production planning to become reactive to the demands. This misalignment became so large that supplies to shelves were getting delayed, and consumers were not getting what they were looking for. The competition jumped in to seize the opportunity and to grab a part of their market share, which they were successful in. Meanwhile, Arvind was trying hard to get the act sorted out, and made many suggestions and reworked plans worked on ways of providing sales forecasting data to production, but found that desired alignment was still not happening. They did manage to improve a little bit, but the market was growing faster, so effectively they were still losing their market share. To add to the misery, new regional competitors started to enter the market too. He was struggling to find a way to get his organization to change gears, and this situation was becoming a major concern, as it was going in the opposite direction of his plan.

Meanwhile, his son, Rajesh (name changes for privacy reasons), had joined the business, after having completed his academic journey and having spent two years visiting all parts of the business, now started to take an active role in the leadership. He had a large consulting company look at the situation and conduct research to advise on the way forward. The advice provided by the consulting company had a few process changes and some organizational structure changes as well. Arvind was quite happy with these ideas, as they also had some logical explanations backing the recommendations, but Rajesh was very apprehensive. The father and son had a meeting, and Rajesh laid out his concerns, where he pointed out that the people in the business would not be comfortable with these changes, and he suggested that we should "seek the opinion" of some of the senior people in the organization about what they think of these recommendations. Arvind conceded to this more to please Rajesh than really thinking of it as a good idea, and sought a meeting with the leadership team.

The eight-member leadership team met in the boardroom at the corporate office along with Arvind and Rajesh making it a group of 10 seated in the air-conditioned boardroom. The room was very well designed, with a mahogany wooden oval table, chairs that had beautiful ornate carvings, and a dark brown fabric seats to contrast the off-white walls, beautiful paintings around on the walls along with a beautifully sculpted statue of Sri Swami Vivekananda in the far right corner of the room, all the needed lighting to highlight the special art pieces in the room was in place too, obviously the work of a very good interior designer. It was also fully equipped with the accessories needed to run group meetings. The meeting started. These eight people, who had been in the company for over ten years, and leading different functions, were in a rather tense state as they were all aware of the way the business was going. They were all expecting some bad news, and the look on their faces said it all. Knowing the father and son, and the culture of the company, they were all secure about their jobs, but yet they were quite tense about what to expect in the meeting - some really bad news perhaps. As Rajesh read out the report and the recommendations, the group quickly accepted these recommended changes. There was also a very clear sigh of relief on many of them, which was also visible. Just as they were about to conclude the meeting, Rajesh sensed that the concurrence to the ideas was very superficial, and he decided to probe a little more.

He then stated – "this report is from the outside in perspective, where an external person was trying to set the right things from their perspective. What would be the perspective looking from the inside? All of you are very experienced, and I am curious to know what your thoughts from your line function perspectives would be and what would be your recommendations to change the current situation?"

The response was a group of people all looking at each other, but no one had anything to say. Rajesh, after a long pause, repeated the ask of them, and told them to think it over, involve their team members if needed, and come up with some ideas, and adjourned the meeting to the next day.

The next day has arrived. The leaders arrived too, and this time one could see a lot of enthusiasm and energy, that now matched the opulently furnished room. Each had some ideas that they shared, and now there was more confusion about which route to take. There was a risk of pleasing one and displeasing the rest, and there was also the factor about how to pick one that is the best of the lot, and at the same time how would everyone agree to that choice.

Fortunately, Rajesh had heard about facilitation as a popular practice, and he announced to the group that they would all reconvene and have an external facilitator run the meeting to arrive at a final plan of action.

The meeting that got arranged a week later brought out some amazing discussions that led to their picking up some ideas, and had the group in consensus to adopt a few changes, which also included some suggestions from the consulting company's recommendations. They were able to create an aligned way of working for all in the organization.

This act of Rajesh, sensing at the right time that the initial agreement was superficial and then getting the group to a consensus via the practice of facilitation saved the company, and today it is once again achieving significant growth and well on its way not only to get to the top but also to stay there.

When I next met Rajesh, I asked him about what made him look at facilitation, and he with a smile and a glint in his eye said – "I learnt that, when you do not know or are in doubt, the best way is to ask." He shared that he was reminded of this saying and he decided to implement it.

Easy enough, isn't it? Whenever we are in doubt, ASK. It is as easy as that. All it needs is an open mind, and the courage to admit that I am in doubt or do not know.

As we take part in meetings that are facilitated and see

methods used to get consensus, we can add those ideas into our repository and use them as needed. The very fact that we are seeking consensus opens up our creative thoughts, and we can come up with various methods ourselves.

What we may need to remind ourselves constantly is that it is a "skill," which means the more we use it, the more we get comfortable with it. At first, it will feel difficult, one can expect to make mistakes and fail too, but continuing to use them and soon you will see yourself getting better, and eventually mastering it. There are other ways to practice in safe environments and learn from other facilitators, and you can do this through by joining a group of facilitators and meeting regularly exchanging ideas and sharing best practices.

In the next chapter, some resources that you can look up and use are shared too.

10
ADDITIONAL RESOURCES

Here are some resources that I found beneficial in my journey of growing as a facilitative leader.

Useful websites:

The International Association of Facilitators – www.iaf-world.org

The ICA International – www.ica-international.org

The Center for Appreciative Inquiry - www.centerforappreciativeinquiry.net

Useful books:

- Facilitation with Ease!, Ingrid Bens
- The Skilled Facilitator, Roger Schwarz
- Spot on Facilitation, Prabu Naidu and Janice Lua

- Designing the Conversation, Ross Unger, Brad Nunnally and Dan Willis
- The Art of Facilitation, Dale Hunter
- The Power of Appreciative Inquiry, David Cooperrider, Diana Whitney, and Amanda Trsoten
- Momentum, Mamie Kanfer Stewart and Tai Tsao
- Essential Facilitation Workbook, Interaction Associates
- How to Lead Work Teams, Fran Rees
- Mission Critical Meetings, Ava S. Butler
- Facilitator's Guide to Participatory Decision-Making, Sam Kaner
- Unlocking the Magic of Facilitation, Sam Killermann and Meg Bolger

Happy facilitating! Enjoy your journey to becoming a successful leader in the VUCA times.

CONCLUSION: TODAY'S LEADERS NEED TO BE GREAT FACILITATORS

We see that there is an evolution to the leadership practices to match with the growth in the hierarchy of needs, and also connected to the environment. These are the core realities before us today, and it is quite evident that what took successful leaders this far, is not going to be adequate to take them further.

By no means, are we writing off the earlier skills developed; those today are a given – communication skills, influencing skills, and value-based leadership; and the era is changing, we are faced with VUCA realities along with the advancement of the needs of the people.

With all these scenarios that we face, most of the problems faced by leaders in today's times can be solved by the deft use of facilitation practices. The practice itself is continuously evolving, and hence leaders should actively get engaged in professional facilitation forums and local chapters. There are many conferences, national, regional, and international; participating in these would also provide some great learning opportunities.

Inspired by a Ted Talk by Shawn Achor – "The Happiness Advantage" who shared some profound thinking, and in line with what he says, the purpose of my writing this book, is to not just have leaders adopt facilitation skills and become better than the average leaders, the goal is to move the entire average up. To be able to do this, we would need the HR community and the Educators to start thinking about these skills as a core competency.

The HR Community have always adopted competency frameworks for a leader as needed, initially it was all about powerful Communicating Skills; there was a little time when Business Acumen took up some importance and got added to the desired leadership competencies list, then Influencing Skills became an important consideration; and a few years ago Memorable Presence took center stage; and now there is a strong business case to add Facilitation Skills. It is time for the HR fraternity to look at how they build this during the journey of their employees too.

The Educators community, have also been closely looking at the industry needs, and some of the best universities have always been quick to adopt new competency needs, and have done it by explicitly teaching those skills, and also giving their students the opportunity to practice them in their tenure in the university, so that they can be industry ready as they graduate.

Circling back, if these two groups, the HR and the Educators start to look at incorporating some of the ideas shared here, the purpose of this book would have been met.

Let's all join together to build a leadership practice that can get better at dealing with the demands of the VUCA environment, let's all be part of the new leadership era.

ABOUT THE AUTHOR

Sanjay Dugar, MBA, CPF, is the Director of C2C Organizational Development Pvt. Ltd.. He is a versatile leader with vast experience in effectively leading companies across different needs.

His out of the box thinking and the attitude to challenge the status quo has seen him succeed in helping grow companies and even turning around some that were not doing well.

Sanjay's domain focus has been largely in the IT and ITeS areas. His peers often call him "Buddha" as he is known to be calm in the most stressful situations and is the "go-to" person during crises that needs immediate resolution.

He attributes his success to his positive attitude, as he often says "B+ is not just my blood group, it is my attitude to life."

Being very passionate about **Helping Leaders Excel**, he has been facilitating many leadership level workshops and works extensively with the HR groups and Educators to see how they can support building great leaders for the future.

His global experience, and extensive research that he has taken up in this area, are shared in the book. He is open to hearing others views on this topic and as his research continues, he is open to sharing his new findings as well.

On a more personal note, he is very fond of sports and loves to participate in any sport that he can manage – in particular, he is fond of badminton, golf, billiards, and cricket.

Lightning Source UK Ltd.
Milton Keynes UK
UKHW012000120521
383610UK00001B/229